The Dynamic Manager's Guide To Marketing & Advertising:

How To Grow Sales
And Boost Your Profits

By Dave Donelson

THE DYNAMIC MANAGER'S GUIDE TO MARKETING & ADVERTISING:
How To Grow Sales and Boost Your Profits

For information, contact Donelson SDA, Inc.
44 Park Lane, West Harrison, NY 10604

FIRST EDITION

ISBN-10: 1453889604
ISBN-13: 9781453889602

Section One is available as an eBook, The Dynamic Manager's Guide To Marketing
Section Two is available as an eBook, The Dynamic Manager's Guide To Advertising

Acknowledgements
Some of the material in this book originally appeared in various forms
in one or more of these publications:

Accessory & Performance Retailer	*Gift Basket Review*
Automotive Aftermarket	*LP Gas Magazine*
Autographics	*NFIB's MyBusiness*
Broadcasting & Cable	*Niche Magazine*
Central NY Business Journal	*NSGA Retail Focus*
The Christian Science Monitor	*Nursery Retailer*
Club Industry	*Performance Business*
Convenience Store Decisions	*Pizza Today*
Distribution Sales & Management	*Professional Builder*
Distribution Channels	*Restyling*
Electronic Media	*Ward's Dealer Business*
Entrepreneur	*Westchester Magazine*
Fabricator	*Woodworker's Journal*
Family Business	*Woodshop News*

Library of Congress Control Number - 2010915608

Table of Contents

About This Book

Businesses come and go and there are plenty of reasons for their success or failure, but the ones that thrive almost always have one thing in common: they are good marketers. What does that mean? It means they make all their business decisions based on meeting their customers' needs. Which products or services they sell, where they sell them, how much they charge for them, how they encourage customers to buy them, and all the other hundreds (if not thousands) of business decisions a good marketer makes start with a simple question: how will this affect my customers?

This customer-first business philosophy isn't something I invented. It's been around since early in the last century when the dynamic managers of their time realized that supplying the kind of widget the customer wanted was more important than how many widgets their factories could produce. In other words, the manager who wanted to grow his business turned his eyes away from the factory floor and started looking outside—at the customers—to figure out how to succeed. Thus began the study and practice of marketing.

Like many people, my introduction to marketing came in college. The classic approach divided the discipline into four elements—the four "P's"—Product, Price, Place, and Promotion. While plenty of academics and others have tried to update, enhance, and expand on this simple scheme, I still feel it's pretty solid. It's probably obvious to you, but here are what the four terms mean:

Product is the "what" of the business—as in "what should we sell?" You probably know that the best answer to this question is "what the cus-

1

tomer wants to buy," but you'd be surprised at how many companies try instead to build a business around "what can we make?" When you ignore the customer's needs and wants, you suffer the fate of the apocryphal buggy whip manufacturer or, to cite a more modern example, you become pets.com, home of the hugely irritating sock puppet mascot and proof that just because you *can* sell kitty litter online doesn't mean you *should*.

Price is market-driven, too, regardless of what your accountant tells you. Sure, you have to cover the cost of your product or service (as well as the overhead of your company) with enough left over to provide a profit, but you won't be able to do that unless the customer is willing to pay for it in the first place. Individual customers don't set your price, but as a group—when they become the market—their judgment of whether you're delivering fair value can't be ignored.

Place deals with the "where" of the business, as in "where does the product come from and where does the customer get it?" This includes topics like supply chain management and product distribution that are a little outside my areas of expertise, so I'll just touch on them lightly in this book.

Promotion covers all the ways you communicate with the customer—from advertising and public relations to how your sales people interact with them in your store, office, telemarketing center, or online. The personal selling facets of marketing are so important I cover them separately in *The Dynamic Manager's Guide To Creative Selling*, but a great deal of this book is about other forms of promotion based on good marketing practices.

My first job in advertising was as a copy writer for a radio station. It didn't pay much, but I learned a ton. Over the years, I produced TV commercials, designed print ads, and planned many media budgets. But you never saw my TV spots on the Super Bowl or my print layouts in Vogue. My clients weren't gigantic multinational brands like Coca-Cola or Chevrolet. Instead, I created ad campaigns for Casey Meyers Ford and Soda Boy (whose still-memorable slogan was "Oh Boy! Soda Boy!"), advertisers in St. Joseph, Missouri, the small town where I grew up. My ads were for local businesses, not national conglomerates. In other words, they promoted businesses just like yours.

Working in local media as I did is a great way to learn a lot about all kinds of businesses. Car dealers, grocery stores, clothing retailers, and home improvement contractors all have different advertising needs. Some are looking for more store traffic, others want to expand their market area. Attracting new customers, building loyalty in the existing clientele, encouraging repeat purchases or introducing new product lines each require different tactics. There are a few principles that apply to them all, but there really is no such thing as one-size-fits-all advertising. Please keep that in mind as you consider the concepts in this book.

When you mention advertising to most people, they immediately think of the behemoths of the airwaves—companies like Procter & Gamble, McDonald's, or Wal-Mart. But big spectacular national ad campaigns like theirs have little in common with advertising the way it's done by small businesses—the kind of advertising you do. In most respects, advertising your business is harder.

Mostly, of course, that's because you don't have a gazillion-dollar advertising budget. You probably don't have a lot of expensive research to precisely define your market or a dedicated psychometric laboratory to test your ads before they run. Your copy writer may double as your store manager most of the time. Your art director most likely spends most of her time freshening merchandise on the shelves. Your media planner? Probably the person who writes the checks—you. In other words, your advertising isn't designed and executed by a team of Madison Avenue gurus, it's the product of the good-hearted people who help make your business a success.

That certainly doesn't mean it isn't effective. Quite frankly, somebody who spends 90% of their time talking to your customers (like your store manager does) is going to have an infinitely better understanding of what they want than some clip-board-toting psychological profiler or white-coated lab technician. You don't need a super computer to calculate your media efficiencies to the fifth decimal point when you're trying to decide whether to promote this year's Father's Day Sale in the *Weekly Inkspot* or the *TV-49 Six O'Clock News*. What you probably do need, though, is a better understanding of what makes advertising effective and how to make it work better for you.

That's where *The Dynamic Manager's Guide To Marketing & Advertising* comes in. This book offers you some basic rules that will help increase the return on your marketing investment. Some of them come from my experiences creating ads and watching customers react to them as I stood in my clients' stores and offices as the campaigns ran. Others were drawn from the lessons learned by small business owners themselves, from auto repair shop owners to nursery retailers, clothing stores to insurance agents. As in all the books in the Dynamic Manager series, much of this material was drawn from my conversations with thousands of small business managers and owners. I filtered their stories through my own experiences as a manager and entrepreneur to distill some sound guidelines on why and how you can market your products and services in the real world. In other words, this book isn't about theory—it's about the real world of small business marketing.

Versions of some of these chapters previously appeared as articles in various national business and trade publications you'll find listed in the bibliography; others were taken from my seminars on marketing. I've also included several case studies of companies that depend on solid marketing to succeed—often against great odds—as well as a few chapters about companies in specialty markets that I found illustrative of good marketing practices. This book contains the full text of two ebooks, *The Dynamic Manager's Guide To Marketing: How To Create And Nurture Your Best Customers* and *The Dynamic Manager's Guide To Advertising: How To Grow Your Business With Ads That Work* as well as additional material in the third section, Promotions And Ad Campaigns You Can Use.

The book is organized to encourage you to sample, think about, and try out different concepts in the daily operation of your business. It's not a narrative or a text book; there isn't a step-by-step organization but rather a collection of useful articles that address practical problems in marketing for small business managers and owners. My goal is simple: to give you some helpful tips and perhaps even some inspiration to become a successful marketer.

-- Dave Donelson

Section One

Marketing:

How To Create And Nurture

Your Best Customers

Chapter 1

Marketing With A Capital "P"

"Before you make any decisions about price,
or which products to sell, or what ads to run,
take a good hard look at your customers as people."

Before you begin applying the four P's of marketing to your business, you need to understand the most important "P" of the discipline. The other four, product, price, place, and promotion, all intersect at one point: People.

"People" as in customers. "People" as in the folks who buy your product or service. It doesn't matter if you are a manufacturer, a retailer, a wholesaler, an inventor, an insurance agent, banker, restaurateur, doctor, lawyer, butcher, baker, or candlestick maker. Without customers, the auto manufacturer's cars turn to piles of rust. Without customers, a farmer's corn rots in the silo. If you don't have a customer, you don't have a business.

And customers, of course, are people. Attracting their attention, persuading them to buy from you, and ensuring their satisfaction with your product or service all require good people skills.

Doing these things really well is how small businesses grow to be big ones. If that is your goal, I urge you to invest your time, energy, and yes, some money, in learning everything you can about the people with whom you do business—your customers. The more you know about what makes them tick, what they want out of life, why they get out of bed in the morning, the more you will know about things like why they buy your product or your competitors', what price might make them change their purchase intentions, and which services they think are important and which ones they find a colossal bother.

The behemoths of marketing, companies like Procter & Gamble and Pepsi, have legions of market researchers to find, dissect, and analyze their customers. They can pay for consumer surveys, finance test products, assemble focus groups, and use dozens of other relatively scientific tools to determine the kinds of things a good marketer wants to know about his customers. As the owner or manager of a small business, you probably don't have those kinds of assets at your disposal. That doesn't mean you have to operate in the dark, however. You can learn almost as much about your customers as they do by turning to that acknowledged expert on almost any subject, your mother-in-law.

Seriously, information gathered through what is known as "mother-in-law research" can be just as valid as the reams of data gathered by P&G's army of white-coated market researchers. It will also be a whole lot cheaper and, even more importantly, it will be much more timely and specific to your business.

Your market research department

"Mother-in-law research" is pretty simple: look around you at your customers and try to spot some patterns in their behavior. If you are observant and objective, you can learn a ton about who they really are and why they act the way they do. As the term implies, you can also learn some interesting things about your customers by asking people who know them—if not your mother-in-law, then your friends, vendors, and employees.

You can get started by making a simple tally of who comes into your store or office during a given week. Are they men or women? How old are they? What would you guess their household income to be? Their education? Blue-collar or white? Are there any other salient facts that might pertain to your particular business like how many cars they own or whether or not they have children? You can often tell a lot by spending some time in your parking lot and watching the people come and go. Keep in mind that you don't have to ask the customer a bunch of questions. Use your powers of observation to make some educated guesses—they'll be close enough.

Another good method is to look at your sales records for a given period. If your data allows, rank individual transactions by profitability (not by gross margin percentage, but by gross profit in total dollars). If gross profit data by transaction isn't available, use the gross sale figure for each one. Credit card transaction records are a good source, although you'll get a more complete picture if you can reconstruct single cash or check transactions as well. Even if you don't have transaction records available, you can use inventory turnover data as a substitute. In that case, rank items by profit volume and try to connect specific customer names to them.

Now make a list of the top 20% of those customers ranked by the size of gross profit they produce. Those are your best customers. According to the justifiably popular 80/20 rule, eighty percent of your gross profit probably comes from them, making them your most profitable customers.

Profile your best customers

Next, do a little above-board sleuthing. Compile your best customers' street addresses from credit card records, phone numbers, delivery destinations, etc. Plot them on a map and look for clusters of them. Good marketers know that birds of a feather flock together; similar people tend to live in similar neighborhoods. Once you've figured out where your best customers live, you can look for other birds of that feather—they're your best new prospects.

Now drive through those neighborhoods. Guesstimate the value of the homes and look at the cars there to get a rough idea of income. Check for kids and/or their bikes, swing sets, and sports equipment (or lack thereof) to get an idea of their parents' ages. Don't limit your surveillance to weekdays, either. Take a few minutes on the weekend to drive through to see how many residents are doing their own yard work or washing their own cars. These things will also tell you a lot about their lifestyle. The more you know about your best customers, the better marketing decisions you will make.

If you are a business-to-business marketer, your research job is actually a little easier. You probably have fewer (but bigger) transactions with fewer customers than someone who sells to the general public, which simplifies your data-gathering. What may complicate it, though, is the tendency for businesses to have multiple decision-makers in their buying processes. Don't be daunted by the details, though—just gather data on one person at a time until you've got a clear picture of who they are and what their role is.

You may also think that personal information like education and lifestyle choices aren't relevant to business buyers since their job is to make rational, profit-oriented purchases. Nothing could be further from the truth. Corporate buyers are people, too, and they allow plenty of emotion to influence their decisions. In fact, a personal, human reaction to a vendor's marketing approach may be the only factor that separates two competitors. The more you know about that business-to-business customer as a person, the greater your chances of tipping their decisions in your favor.

So, before you make any decisions about price, or which products to sell, or what ads to run, take a good hard look at your customers as people. Identifying your best customer takes some work. The end result, though, is marketing that works better, costs less, and generates greater profits.

Chapter 2
How Many Baskets For How Many Eggs?

"An emotion-free analysis of each segment of the business is a good place to start."

One of the most difficult—and important—decisions any business operator has to make is whether to specialize or to generalize. Should you try to be all things to all customers or seek out and serve only a specific market niche? It may seem so, but it's not an easy choice to make.

In some ways, the route to specialization is easier to follow and the reasons to take it are more compelling. You may have particular skills and experience that lend themselves to one type of service work, or a real eye for style and fashion that makes you a genius when it comes to buying merchandise, as well as a reputation in that market that will help you bring in the business. You and your crew may have superb expertise in fine cabinetry, for example, and the tools and inventory to compete with the best in turning dowdy kitchens into visual masterpieces, but lack the practiced touch of a master glazer (not to mention the shop space and equipment) necessary to create custom ceramic tile. If that's the case, it only makes sense to play to your strengths and concentrate on the cabinet business.

The payoff of specialization can be large because, if you work at it, you can grow to dominate your niche by trading on your reputation for outstanding workmanship. As your dominance grows, you'll probably be able to charge slightly higher prices and amortize your fixed costs over a larger revenue stream, two factors that will substantially increase your profitability.

In an ideal world, your small competitors won't be able to economically compete, and you'll have all the business you can handle.

Specialized dangers

Few of us operate in an ideal world, however, and there are downside risks in becoming too specialized. Consider the cabinet maker again. That is, after all, a type of fashion business with all the marketing uncertainties that word implies. What are you going to do with all those hand-forged hinges and handles if the rough-hewn rustic look goes out of style next year? Or what will happen to your Italian marble counter top monopoly if most of the home owners in your market decide they prefer faux granite?

Like more and more businesses these days, yours is also probably driven by technology, which changes relentlessly. The business owner or manager who doesn't keep up with the latest technological advances is going to find him or herself with empty aisles and a storeroom full of unsold inventory. The problem, of course, is that technology mutates exponentially, making it harder and harder to keep up with what's coming down the pike and making forecasting errors more and more expensive to correct. If you think it can't happen, ask yourself whatever happened to all those CB radios, eight-track players, and avocado-colored appliances.

So, to return to our cabinet shop example, should you strive to be a full-service home remodeler? Sure! All you need to do is find a 5,000-sq.-ft. building and fill it with tools and equipment, hire plumbers, painters, carpenters, upholsterers, electricians, designers, glass cutters, a few general gofers, and some really wild creative types of unknown expertise, finance a 10,000-sq.-ft. warehouse full of specialized inventory, hang out a shingle, and you're in business! While you're at it, why not throw in a retail showroom and a few good salespeople? Simple, huh?

General confusion

Generalization has its drawbacks, too, obviously, including high set-up costs that can be difficult to amortize. An auto body paint booth that is used once a week costs the same as one that is used once a day, which makes the profit on that once-a-week job pretty slim. And let's not even talk about the salary of the guy who wields the spray gun. How does he contribute to the bottom line when he's standing around waiting for the next job to pull in?

It's also tough to be really good at a lot of different things, which makes it harder to totally satisfy every customer. That, in turn, can lead to a reputation for less-than-stellar service and the resultant lukewarm word-of-mouth that goes along with it. The daily management headaches multiply with generalization, too, along with the wider variety of employee skill sets required, not to mention the greater number of project problems that can arise. The solution for most business owners lies somewhere in between.

The middle path

The smart operators don't put all of their eggs in one basket, as tempting as that may be, nor do they spread themselves too thin. A business that focuses on one *type* of work or stocks particular, related lines of merchandise probably has the best chance to combine the advantages and minimize the drawbacks of both approaches. You can diversify your business enough to cope with the vagaries of technology and style while specializing enough in one area to have a good run at dominating the market for it.

An auto shop that concentrates on interiors, for example, can combine several disciplines that have inter-related skills, tools, and equipment. Upholsterers can generally handle carpeting while audio installers may also be able to put in instrumentation and gauges. Such an operation can also be very successful at selling add-ons because the customer is pre-disposed to upgrading that area of their vehicle already. Plus, of course, the shop owner can probably show the customer some price advantages of doing multiple jobs simultaneously. Selling a set of dash and door inserts to the customer who's come in for new seat covers should be an automatic.

Homegrown or outsourced?

Even the most dedicated general we-do-it-all companies nearly always send at least some of their work out to subcontractors. In fact, as the technology in some fields becomes more demanding, outsourcing is often the only way the job can get done economically.

That strategy can help the specialist perform more like a generalist, too. A sunroof installer, for example, might sell a customer new seat covers, too, by contracting the upholstery work out to a strategic partner. He doesn't need to deceive the customer about where the work is done, either, since the main things most of them care about (after quality) are that the price is right and the work is guaranteed.

The principal contractor (the sunroof installer in this example) should be willing to stand behind the upholstery job, which means finding another subcontractor if necessary, and should price it at no more than what the customer could get it done for if bought directly. The upholsterer, in other words, is going to need to forego some profit in return for getting additional work.

There is no one prescription that applies to every business when it comes to deciding how much specialization is enough and how much generalization is too much. An emotion-free analysis of each segment of the business based on actual sales and profitability data is a good place to start, though. That should be followed by a similarly-objective inventory of skills the staff currently has and a hard look at the potential market for each service or product line under consideration. Once the facts are on the table, then it's time to make a decision.

Chapter 3
Case Study:
Conwin Carbonic Inflates An Industry

"Conwin transformed itself
from a product-driven industrial operation
to a customer-driven marketing company."

Many companies change direction when they transfer control from one generation to the next, but few turn the steering wheel as sharply as Conwin Carbonic. Once an industrial gas supplier in the Los Angeles market, the company is now a leading player in balloon entertainment around the world. In its early days, Conwin sold prosaic CO_2 regulators used in restaurant beverage dispensers; today they shower party-goers with confetti from exploding balloons. Under the leadership of second-generation-owner Michael Wing, Conwin transformed itself from a product-driven industrial operation to a customer-driven marketing company.

Even though it eventually involved nearly every aspect of the company's business, Conwin's transformation wasn't the result of heavy number-crunching, in-depth market projections, or extensive financial analysis. "It was a very evolutionary decision," Michael says. "Knowing this was going to be my company, that's the direction I wanted to go."

The changes began innocently enough when founder Al Wing, an insatiably curious engineer, invented a device to inflate large numbers of balloons more precisely and efficiently. To Al, it was just one more engineering problem neatly solved; to Michael, it was opportunity incarnate. "Dad didn't just build a better mouse trap," Michael says, "He invented the mouse trap."

Helping people scratch their noses

In a way, Conwin got its start in adversity. Not long after Al received his degree in civil engineering from USC, he came down with Guillain-Barré Syndrome, a disorder of the nervous system that can cause paralysis of the legs, arms, and other parts of the body. He entered Rancho Los Amigos Hospital where he became fascinated by the devices used in rehabilitation. After he overcame his illness, Al went to work with the institution's research group making what he terms "artificial muscles powered by carbon dioxide" to assist invalids, many of whom suffered from polio. "We gave people an opportunity to do some basic things for themselves like scratch their nose and comb their hair," Al explains.

Regulators that control the flow of gases were important components in such devices, but they had other applications as well. Al secured distribution rights for a regulator and started Conwin Carbonic with his wife, Alberta, in the garage of their Whittier, California, home in 1960. With Alberta managing the office and Al running production, they sold regulators and CO2, largely to restaurants for beverage dispensers. Over time, they expanded their product line to include high-pressure cylinders and other gases including helium, oxygen, and nitrogen. Dry ice grew into a big part of the business and Conwin became a major supplier to nearby Hollywood studios, where tons of it was used for special effects. *Ghost Busters* was one of their biggest projects, according to Michael.

The Wings' eldest daughter, Patty, introduced balloons into the family lexicon in the 70's when she opened her own business, 'Balloons by Patty,' one of Los Angeles' first balloon decorating companies. The balloon industry was in its infancy and Al recognized a challenge as Patty described her struggles with existing technology. "We saw that there was a need for equipment that would be more user friendly," he says. "The regulators that were used at that time were borrowed from the welding industry. They performed the function okay but they didn't lend themselves to balloons very well."

Million balloon extravaganzas

Al's first innovative breakthrough was the Dual Split-Second Sizer, a high-speed multi-nozzle inflator that reduced the time needed to produce large-scale balloon displays. The product revolutionized the industry by making it possible to stage million-balloon extravaganzas at conventions, parties, sporting events and concerts such as those for Bette Midler and The Rolling Stones.

Patty was killed in a tragic auto accident with a drunk driver, but her foray into the balloon business had already left its mark on Conwin. Michael, ten years younger than Patty, recalls having great fun as a boy helping her out on opening day during the balloon release at Dodger Stadium. When he graduated from Pepperdine University in 1985, he joined Conwin as its first VP of Marketing with a head full of aggressive ideas for growing the balloon business. At that time it still represented less than half of the company's total revenues, but it was growing rapidly.

Al says with pride, "I didn't develop the business like Mike has. He has the vision and the energy."

Balloons were the future for Michael. "The industrial side of our business was easy, but there wasn't much growth potential," he says. "It was pretty much tapped out." They sold the dry ice business, which provided a third of their revenues at the time, to a competitor in 1987. Michael says the low-growth, labor-intensive dry ice operation didn't fit his vision of the future and diverted time, energy, and funds from the growing balloon business.

Conwin still serves the industrial gas industry and provides specialized but low-volume equipment like nitrogen dispensers for wine bars, pneumatic regulators used in vineyards and auto racing, and medical devices like the insufflator, which pumps carbon dioxide into a body cavity to give the surgeon room to work during laparoscopic surgery and other procedures. Today, that division represents about twenty percent of total sales. Products are designed and manufactured for other companies, who market them under their own labels.

"We never made a decision to not market to the industrial side of the business," Michael explains. "It is very turnkey in many ways. People come to us and ask for something with this connection and that setting and this style gauge and that output pressure. It's just that more and more of our energies went into the balloon industry." Conwin didn't turn away from the industrial gas business; the balloon business simply outpaced it.

Innovation from customer feedback

Growth in the balloon business was fueled by a stream of innovative products Al designed based on feedback gathered by Michael from balloon decorators, party planners, event coordinators, and other participants in the rapidly expanding industry. Balloons may be the ultimate non-digital one-piece toy, but the products that put Conwin on the map are anything but simple. From automatic shut-off foil balloon inflators to pneumatic balloon exploders, low-temperature fluorescent balloon light bulbs, and pneumatic cannons that spew more than a pound of confetti in one blast, Conwin's equipment raises balloon "fun" to a higher level. All products are manufactured in the US, although most production is outsourced to provide greater response to spikes in demand and preclude the necessity to invest in expensive, high-tech machine tools. Conwin employs about 40 people.

What Conwin brought to the industry was efficiency. The revolutionary products Al designed enabled balloon artists to create intricate, large-scale displays using thousands of balloons and spectacular special effects. Before he invented the multi-nozzle regulator with a foot pedal control, for example, each worker inflated one balloon at a time from a cylinder of gas. Gas cylinders are very heavy and awkward to handle, so you don't want to haul around any more than you absolutely have to. "One worker tying up one tank doesn't make a lot of sense," Michael says. "The three-operator regulator was the home run." It allows three people to work from one tank of gas simultaneously.

"It was a huge breakthrough," Michael continues. "Generally on a balloon job, one of the constraints is time. The wedding or the party is in a public facility like a country club or banquet hall that's booked with back-to-back events. There will be just a little time in between to set up. You can't build these large balloon structures off-site because of the logistics. With equipment that's very efficient (and fast and easy) producing consistent results, you can have an inexperienced worker do it."

Balloon decorators don't have big staffs. They might have a small party one weekend where they need two extra hands and a wedding the next where they need ten. The workers are often inexperienced friends and family, so the precision needs to be built into the tools, not trained into the workers.

Al's inventions also improved architectural effects like balloon columns and arches. According to Michael, these are created by tying two balloons together with a square knot. That's called a duplet. You twist two duplets together, then keep stacking them on the line and you can build anything, he says. If the balloons aren't inflated to exactly the same size, though, they look like a bad ear of corn with different-sized teeth. "We use solenoid valves that are very, very, very precise to the tenth of a second," Michael explains. "You can set it and work really quickly." It takes about two seconds to blow up an eleven inch balloon. One person can inflate while another one ties them together.

Launching an industry

These innovations helped launch a cottage industry that Entrepreneur Magazine calls one of the top self-employment opportunities available. "One thing I've always felt good about is that we have given all kinds of people opportunities," observes Michael's mother, Alberta Wing. "For a few bucks, they can get a cylinder and a few balloons and they're in business! I've seen plenty of people who start out in that very small way—working with church groups and such—and now they've got great businesses. I take great pleasure in that."

By 1988, Conwin was a major distributor of balloons as well as a manufacturer of the equipment used to inflate them and produce special effects. They moved into a new facility devoted almost entirely to what was then their principal business, balloons. Michael's wife, Dee, a visual merchandiser by trade, designed a store-like space to streamline the growing traffic. "It's a wholesale store with aisles and shopping carts. It's visually pleasing," Michael says. Big bins hold the merchandise and colorful displays encourage decorators to touch and see the product. "When a balloon is flat, it's nothing," Michael observes. "When you blow it up, it takes on a whole new dimension and life. You've got to have a lot of products on display." The entire facility is 40,000 square feet, with 6,000 devoted to the cash-and-carry side. There is also a big display window. There are about 3,000 SKU's in the store. Ribbons, decorating accessories, and other special items round out the inventory.

There is some retail trade, Michael says, but Conwin is not geared to it because products are sold in large lots, like bags of 100 balloons, although they do offer some rental equipment for schools and other groups. Pricing is also tiered to encourage volume purchasing. The store caters to buyers in a 15-mile radius in the LA area, where they have over 5,000 customers. Conwin works through a network of 40 distributors in the US, most of whom are in the party goods business, and sells an ever-increasing amount of merchandise over the Internet through two websites, www.conwinonline.com and www.laballoons.com. The domestic sales staff consists of four people who handle in-house support for distributors.

Conwin dominates the small but growing balloon industry. The market includes paper and party retailers, entertainment and corporate event coordinators, rental outlets, florists, and entrepreneurial balloon designers. Balloons are used for event decor, gift bouquets, sculptures and installations, and in spectacular special effects using confetti, synchronized explosions, and mass releases. There are also the ever-popular balloon animals made from twisted wiener-shaped balloons. There is even a niche in the fashion industry devoted to apparel made from balloons. According to *Party and Paper Magazine*, balloons and balloon accessories are the top two product categories in the $8.5 billion party and paper industry. "It's a small, niche market," Michael explains. "From a competitive standpoint, we estimate we have over a 70% share of the market worldwide."

The domestic market is growing about five percent annually, Michael says, but the international market is just developing. Since Conwin sells products that will help the growth of the balloon industry in other countries like it did in the US, it's well-positioned to profit from that expansion. To develop the international business, Michael hired fulltime employees who live and work overseas. The international accounts manager and her staff is based in London and manages all sales in Europe. He worked out a warehousing deal with a partnering manufacturer in England to serve as a fulfillment center. A third of revenue comes from international customers now. "I foresee within the next five years, it will be forty to fifty percent of our business. The potential overseas is tremendous," Michael says. The company has a sales manager in Kuala Lumpur for Asia and another in Guadalajara that handles Latin America.

Customer-centric innovations

Other efficiencies for both Conwin and its customers are found online. "The Internet is playing a huge role in our business," Michael says. "In January, we launched a DVD in six languages and put it on the web as well as packing hard copies with key products. People can go right there and watch the product in action." The web has also cut down on the need for staffing. "You can download instruction streets, warranty information, service and support. It's streamlined so many things," he says. Outstanding balloon artists are showcased on the website, too.

Another customer-centric innovation is the Conwin Balloon Design Academy, which offers seminars covering topics like "Wedding Décor Wonders" and "The Business of Bar/Bat Mitzvahs." The three-hour classes draw about thirty students who pay $35 to $50 to attend. There's always a break for student mixing and networking, which is also a big draw. In addition, Michael says, "Students get promotional coupons for the equipment we use in the classes. They go right from the classroom down to the store, which is in the same location."

Conwin partners with one of the leading balloon manufacturers, Qualitex, who certifies balloon designers when they complete an extensive training program. The CBA designation is similar to FTD for florists, which allows customers to order balloon designs from coast to coast.

The Wing family has transformed their business from a stolid, stable concern to a company that literally manufactures fun. When you blow up a bright red balloon, a child's face lights up with joy. Fill it with helium so it dances in the air, and their eyes fill with wonder. Release a half-million multicolored balloons into the sky, and even the adults in the crowd will clap their hands with glee. Conwin Carbonic is one of the few companies whose products bring that kind of happiness into the world. With a product that's synonymous with good times, it's easy to understand why. As Alberta says, "If you're going to spend your life in a business, you should have a little fun."

Originally published in *Family Business*, www.familybusinessmagazine.com

Chapter 4

How Niche Is Your Market?

*"Serving a special market successfully requires
paying particular attention to customer communication."*

The last man who envisioned the automotive market as a homogenous mass was Henry Ford, and it didn't take him long to realize that selling one model in one color to satisfy every single customer wasn't the best possible business plan. Most modern markets are no different, with a seemingly ever-growing list of market niches that the savvy service provider or retailer can serve.

Just like Henry Ford, though, it's not possible for a business owner to be everything to everybody. You need to specialize, at least to some extent, in order to maximize the return on your investment in facilities, parts, and equipment, not to mention the demands on your technical knowledge.

Selling to each market requires a specialized knowledge base, too, since the customers in each one are motivated differently. If you are in the automotive aftermarket, for example, you know that the people who build and drive nitrous-powered dragsters aren't generally the same ones who tear around dirt ovals in restored 1930's roadsters. And the baby boomer replicating his '55 Chevy dream machine differs greatly from his son or daughter bolting some speed onto their first Honda Civic.

As Chris Sutton, owner of the Street Rod Garage in Grant, Alabama, says, "You've got people that are original equipment freaks most of the time on the restoration side of it. You couldn't give them a street rod. But street rods guys, you couldn't give them an original."

Sell what you know for customers you know

Most small business owners follow their own interest into the niche markets they serve. It's a natural choice, since they tend to know what people like themselves are going to want and have the technical expertise to provide it. Beyond that though, serving a special market successfully requires paying particular attention to customer communication.

John Pruitt, owner of John's Rod Shop in Abbeville, South Carolina, has been studying his customer base for a long time and understands them very well. "Generally, my customer who builds a car is in his late forties or better," he says. "They want to reach back and touch that nostalgia. They say, 'I had one of those when I was a kid, or Dad had one of those, and I'd like to have one.'"

Pruitt's shop builds street rods from the ground up as well as performing maintenance and repair on muscle cars, modifieds, or early model speedsters. He follows a strict routine with his customers. "The first thing I try to find out when a customer calls me is what kind of car are they looking for," he says. "The second thing we want to know is what they want the car to do for them. Do they want a car they can get in and drive to California and be comfortable at interstate speeds? Or do they want to build a street bruiser that they can get out here and drive like a race car?"

This process doesn't stop after the initial meeting. Pruitt adds, "As you complete the project, you have to be in continual contact with that customer so he knows what's going on and he knows where his money's going."

The extreme niche market

Andy Voytilla, owner of Dream Machines in Lake Oswego, Oregon, serves a very different niche market—one that almost defines the term. He specializes in antique race car restoration and rebuilds of racing stock as old as the 1920's—what were known, depending on the region, as speedsters or strip-downs and that often ran on borrowed horse race tracks. He draws most of his customers from the local clubs to which he belongs and has supported over the years, so he knows them well.

One of these is the Northwest Vintage Speedsters, whose members own 1934 and earlier 4-cylinder cars. These early hot rods, even those raced on dry lakes and the track roadsters of the '30's and '40's, were driven on the street when they weren't racing. In the past, the club met at his shop. There are about 30 active local members, although there are about 190 members in total including many from Canada and Europe. He works on 12 to 15 club member cars per year and gets so much business from the club that he has little time to handle other work. The club does timed road races, a 100-mile race on Memorial Day and a 200-miler on Labor Day, as well as hill climbs and drag events, so repair work is often called for.

One problem with serving a niche like this, according to Voytilla, is that enthusiasts are drawn to cars about ten years older than they are ('20's-era speedsters appeal to gear heads well into their Social Security years), so the group is constantly diminishing.

Marketing to youngsters

Younger automotive performance enthusiasts make up a particularly difficult market for many shop owners to serve profitably. As Pruitt points out, "The Honda Civic that that teenager's driving out there is comparable to our generation's '55 Chevy. Unfortunately, usually those guys don't have the money."

"A lot of those guys want to buy every part over the Internet, and we can't compete with the Internet pricing," he observes. "These young guys are real savvy and they do a lot of the work themselves or they have a buddy do it because they don't have the money to pay a professional shop."

But that's not to say they should be ignored. As Pruitt says, "That market has got to be acknowledged, massaged, and worked with in order for this industry to grow and survive."

Voytilla says that customer communication is essential. "When a customer comes to me to build a car, the big trick is to get into their mind and see their vision, because a lot of people can't communicate well enough to tell you exactly what they want." It helps when the customer has some hands-on experience with cars, so Voytilla encourages them to take part in the project in some way: "I always encourage my customers to come by the shop on a regular basis. Quite often I even get them to chase parts for me because when they get involved it is easier to get their ideas into it and make it like they wanted it."

Neither Pruitt or Voytilla do any media advertising because they feel their reputation in their market niches is strong enough to pull in plenty of work. That's not to say they do absolutely no marketing, however, because their constant attendance at car shows, cruise-ins, rallies, races, and other events serves to put their work in front of plenty of people. The drawback to that strategy, of course, is that it doesn't reach many new-to-the-market customers.

In a way, though, that's not particularly important to the shop owner who is more interested in serving a particular group of enthusiasts than in growth for growth's sake. If the market niche is big enough, it can support a shop quite well for many years.

Chapter 5

Seven Ways To Wow Your Customers

"Surprises work really well when they come later,
after the customer has started to forget
the last time they did business with you."

If you want to keep your customers coming back to your business, give them a surprise. Do something unexpected for them, and your name will earn a prominent place in their mental filing cabinet securely placed with "Stores to return to" and "Service providers to recommend."

The surprise you give your customers doesn't have to be a big one. In fact, it's the small touches that resonate with meaning, that make them feel like their order is more than just another job on your list. In fact, it was a little thing that sparked this idea for me. We got a Christmas card from Ed Plante Auto Detailing last year. The card wasn't anything special, but there was a surprise inside that made it stand out from all the other business associates' holiday greetings we received: he included a picture of our family SUV taken after his last detailing. In other words, he surprised us with a small, personal touch that made us feel just a tiny bit special.

When you do a little something extra like Ed did, you acknowledge your customer as a friend, as someone whose good feelings toward you warrant particular attention. The picture itself wasn't any big deal either, but, as your mother always said, it's the thought that counts.

The main factor to keep in mind is that what you do needs to be slightly out of the ordinary, something the customer doesn't expect. That means it doesn't have to occur at the point of service; in fact, surprises work really well when they come later, after the customer has started to forget the last time they did business with you. Secondly, the surprise should have a personal angle to it. If it's something you do for every customer, like the book store clerk who automatically puts a bookmark in the bag with every order, it's not going to prompt anybody to give it a second thought.

Different kinds of businesses present all sorts of opportunities to give customers great surprises. The picture Ed sent was of our clunky old family SUV with a fresh wax job. Can you imagine what kind of impact an unexpected picture of an auto restyler customer's tricked-out rides would have? Those customers' cars mean a lot or they wouldn't be spending money on them. To the auto shop customer, getting a picture of his car is like getting a picture of his kids—maybe better!

Surprises online

If you want to go an extra step, you can really "wow" the customer by putting a picture of the results of your work for them on a calendar, coffee mug, t-shirt, or even a teddy bear. If you do home remodeling, painting, landscaping, pool installations, or anything else with a visual impact, a customer gift will be a real treat. Online services like Café Press (www.cafepress.com) will put your digital photo on a wide variety of merchandise for just a few dollars. There aren't any setup charges and you can order a piece at a time, too. All it takes is a photo and a few minutes online.

While you're cruising the web with marketing on your mind, look for websites, groups, or other online material your customer might find interesting. Then drop him or her an email with a link to the site you've found. If your customer is a Corvette owner, for example, send him a link to the nearest Corvette club's website. Even if he already belongs, he'll appreciate the fact that you were thinking of him. Just about every special interest group you can imagine is on the Internet someplace. It doesn't have to be anything exotic, either. If you know your customer is into music, send her a link to an up-and-coming band's MySpace site. It should go without saying that you need to know your customer to carry out this tactic.

The key factor is to make your surprise something with a personal connection to the individual customer. If your nursery sends a generic link to all the flower shows in your area to all your customers, that's fine, but you've lost that personal touch that makes the surprise such a potent marketing tool. Never forget, you're in the retail business, where you succeed by selling one customer at a time.

Speaking of websites, what's on yours? It's fine to have pages extolling the virtues of your experience, the value of your merchandise, and the expertise of your technicians, but you're missing a bet if you don't have a section devoted to your customers. For a mechanic, putting a picture of your customer's car on the web is like taping their kid's picture to the refrigerator door. It makes you both feel good. Just don't post any identifying information about the customer on the web: a caption describing the car and perhaps the work you did on it is enough. And never, ever, post a picture of the customer's kid on the Internet—with or without permission.

Once the picture is up, surprise him with the link in an email. These days, you don't even have to pay for a website. The social networks like Facebook or MySpace, photo sharing sites like Flickr, Shutterfly, and Ko-dak.com or even blog services such as Google's Blogger, are all free and can allow you to communicate with—and surprise—your customers online.

Significant others

Another person who likes surprises is the customer's significant other. While she (or he, as the case may be), may not be the one who decides their home entertainment center needs a new subwoofer, digital server, or gaming system, they may very well be the one who pays the bill. You want them on your side—or at least not working against you. For a couple of bucks, you can send a box of candy or a few flowers. For a few dollars less, you can give their kid a music-themed coloring book. Remember when you got a lollipop at the doctor's office after you got a shot? For a few cents, it took your mind off the sting.

You don't have to spend money on merchandise to give your customer a pleasant surprise, though. Another way is to do something unexpected for them at the time of service. If you operate an auto repair garage, you may or may not automatically wash the customer's car when you're finished—but you can. You can also take a few minutes to vacuum the interior or give the tires a quick wipe with a sidewall compound. If you really want to give the customer a thrill, call when the job is done and offer to deliver the car so they don't have to pick it up. Or, a couple of weeks after the car is out of the shop, call to make sure everything's all right.

If you want to keep your customers coming back, surprise them. The unexpected email message, note or card, gift, or service not only reminds them that you're there, but says you're interested in them as individuals. It's a way to extend the hand of friendship without a bill in it. You'll create goodwill and reinforce their positive opinion of your work, which will lead to more referrals and repeat business. In the end, you will be surprised at the way your sales grow.

Chapter 6
Specialty Market Case Study:
Selling To Off-Roaders

"The amount of time we spend with the customer
is our competitive advantage."

One of the biggest, fastest-growing segments of the automotive performance industry is the off-road market, but beware of approaching it as if
it were a monolithic mass. As industry veteran Rusty Megois says, "I could
talk to twenty off-roaders and they'd each have different interests."

The market ranges from axle-busting rock crawlers and dust-eating
dune racers to soccer moms whose grill-guarded, suspension-jacked, fog-
lighted SUV's never touch any surface rougher than the gravel drive at their
weekend home at the lake. Each customer is different, but they've all got
wallets ready to open to trick out their 4WD ride.

"The off-road market is a lot more diversified," observes Megois, who
started his off-road parts and service business, Rusty's Off-Road in Rain-
bow City, Alabama, in 1976. "You've got guys from sixteen years old to
retirees. You've also got a lot more women interested these days."

Jim Daley, who owns a shop specializing in extreme vehicles in Brew-
ster, New York, says, "The term off-road has become a stereotype of the
rock crawler rolling down the mountainside. What about the guy in Mon-
tauk who runs on the beach? Or the guy in Vermont who can't get up his
driveway because they don't plow it? We put the winch on the front, and
the three-inch lift kit, and the 33-inch all-terrains, and the lockers, with a

Thule rack on top and a nav unit. They're just as important as the guy who buys a three-inch Terra Flex kit."

What differentiates these customers from each other is the way they use their off-road vehicle. What's usually the same is what they want from the shop they choose: knowledgeable service.

Getting to know the customer

"You've got the customer who knows the product, and he doesn't want to talk to somebody who doesn't know anything," Megois says. "Then you've got the other guy who has done the Internet research, read the magazines, but they're still not sure. They rely a lot on what you tell them."

That's why shop and off-road park owner Carl Roy says he and his staff don't sell anybody anything. Instead, "We explain things like the importance between differential ratio and tire size, weight balance and distribution, ground clearance, approach and departure angles, wheel speed versus the inertia of the vehicle." He operates Performance Off-Road, Inc., in Alexandria, Kentucky.

Roy stresses the importance of learning as much as you can about the individual customer: "When it comes to what they want, it depends on their level of experience. For some of them, name recognition means a great deal, there's a certain amount of brand loyalty. Others, it may come down to who had the best magazine ad that month."

The hard-core customer still sets the standard for the market, even though there are vast differences from one to another in that market segment and their tastes are changing, too. There is still the axle-buster, according to Daley, who spends his money on performance. "If the body is caved in, he doesn't care. He'll spend $10,000 on an axle before he'll spend $50 on a flare." Others, though, "Want a little bit nicer rim and tire," he says. "They want the nicer flare. They want things painted now, whereas before black spatter coat was the standard. Now these trucks are thirty-five to forty thousand dollars and they want the bling."

"Five years ago, they wanted function," Megois adds. "Now the parts also have to look trick."

Price doesn't seem to be as much of a concern to off-road customers as it is in other performance markets, although it's always there in the customer's mind somewhere. Megois, who manufactures parts, retails on the web, and services customer trucks, says that "Price isn't nearly as important as it used to be. Now, people want the parts. We can see that in shipping. They're not afraid to pay extra to get it quick."

Marketing off the web

"The Internet has made us all more competitive," Megois says, "but there are a lot of sellers out there who go and come. There are a lot of guys sitting in their underwear in their basement making people think they're a huge corporation. They usually sell too cheap and they don't have the experience. They last six to eighteen months and they disappear."

"With everybody operating these websites and selling this stuff, it can become a price-based issue," Roy says, but he doesn't mind it at all. "The Internet gives us a focal point to start the discussion. A lot of people will come in with an ad they've printed out and say 'I'd like this for my Jeep. Can you beat that price?' That creates the opportunity for us to take them out and illustrate that there are differences—qualitative differences, warranty differences, product support differences, engineering philosophies—and how those transcend the price points of the product."

Roy's staff spends a lot of time with customers on the company's own test trails and RTI ramps. "To give them a real hands-on," he says, "we'll put them in a vehicle and take them out on a trail if they want to see how to use a winch, or what this bumper will do for them, or how much suspension flex this thing has. We take them out and show them right there on the spot."

It's a time-consuming process, but it pays off. As he points out, "If we can take someone out and let them use something like this prior to purchasing it, it already justifies the expense."

Advertising starts the process

All three of these shop owners believe in aggressive advertising to bring in new customers. They use national magazines, web sites, local publications, and even television to get the word out. In addition, they're active in event-based marketing. Megois has a 48-foot parts trailer that made stops at twenty shows and rallies last year. Roy does a trail ride every season to raise money for charity from sponsors, entry fees, and raffle tickets, as well as a car show where all the entry fees go to charity. "It does the community good and lets the community see us," he says.

Once they get the customer through the door, though, the real marketing begins. That's when they start to build a relationship that repeatedly makes the cash register ring. "The average good customer who is building a truck, we see three to five times a year for three or four years," Daley observes.

Roy agrees: "We realize they buy one part this month, next month they're going to do something else, the next month they're going to ask somebody for something for Christmas. We like to be sure what they're buying will work together synergistically and they can build on those. I don't think there's a down-side to that."

"The amount of time we spend with the customer is our competitive advantage," Roy says. "Everybody out there is selling the same stuff we are. The only advantages we offer are the experience and abilities we have."

Chapter 7

First Impressions

*"Take a look around and try to see the place
the way customers see it."*

What is the first thing your customers see when then come to your store or office? No, this isn't a rhetorical question—what kind of first impression do you make?

First impressions are lasting impressions. They affect both your relationships with existing customers and the likelihood of closing the sale to new ones. Beauty may be only skin deep, but most customers don't have x-ray eyes, so that's all they see. What your shop, your employees, and yes, even you, look like is surprisingly important to the success of your business. So take a look around and try to see the place the way customers see it.

What you want, of course, is to present your business as a place where professionals work with pride. Most customers don't expect someplace like a furniture refinishing shop to be pristine, but they quickly draw a relationship between what the place looks like and the quality of work they can expect to get. If the shop is neat and organized, they'll assume their job will run smoothly. If the technicians look like they care about their personal appearance and hygiene, the customer will believe they will take equal pride in the work they do. A clean, professional shop environment gives the customer confidence in the quality of the work.

The opposite is also true, of course. If your office looks like it's about to go out of business—burnt-out bulbs in the light fixtures, discarded packing material surrounded by waist-high weeds in the parking lot, footprints in the dust on the floor—the customer may be just a little reluctant to turn over their treasured heirloom to you for a weeks-long restoration, especially if you ask for a good-sized down payment on the job.

Look and feel like a pro

Besides customer confidence, though, there are other benefits to keeping a clean, well-ordered shop. For one, such facilities are usually much more efficient. Everybody knows where the tools are, what parts are in stock and where to find them, where to find the paperwork as the job progresses. They also build morale in the technical and office staff. Most of us prefer a work environment that looks professional because it makes us feel like pros, too.

So what should your shop look like? Take a look around and apply a little common sense.

Look outside first. Does your shop bear even a slight resemblance to Fred Sanford's front yard? If so, you've got a problem. It's tough to keep a shop storage lot clean when there are half-finished jobs that need to be kept there. A little screening to keep the parking lot separate from the storage lot with some bushes or a fence can help the situation. While you're at it, check the parking lot (or on-street spaces) for trash and litter, too.

It's also a good idea to make sure your signage presents your best image, too. Is it faded or scratched up? Assuming that's not how you want your name to be remembered, invest in new signs or have the old ones refurbished. And don't forget to check the lights both on the signs and your building. Then take a look at the windows—when was the last time they were cleaned?

See through the customer's eyes

Now come inside where the real fun begins. When a customer comes through the door, what's the first thing they see? A desk piled with catalogs, work orders, and old pizza boxes? A counter cluttered with loose parts and half-full cups of cold coffee? If they lean against it, will they stick to it? Obviously, these don't reflect the impression you want to make on a prospective customer—or an existing one you want to come back often.

Areas where customers visit—waiting room, service counter, your desk—should be well-lit, clean, and uncluttered. If there is merchandise on display, it should certainly not have a coat of dust on it. And do I need to even mention the restrooms?

Even if customers aren't allowed into the shop, they'll go there if you give them half a chance. When they do, they should find an area with a total air of professionalism about it. No one expects a shop to meet operating-room standards, but they'll be really, really impressed if it comes close. A spotless, perfect shop sends the message that you perform spotless, perfect work.

Finally, take a look at the staff—and yourself. Uniforms aren't necessary, but clean clothes certainly are. What customer wants some technician's greasy butt print on his newly upholstered chair? Then there's the touchy matter of grooming. While long hair and artisanship seem to go together just fine, clean long hair works even better when it comes to impressing the customer with your staff's standards of hygiene—and work. The same holds true for facial adornments.

This may seem like a lot of prissy Felix Unger stuff, but it's not. A clean, orderly, organized business will make the kind of first—and second, and third—impression that attracts more money to your cash register.

Chapter 8
Welcome All Newbies

"Remember what it was like when you went
onto the field for your very first Little League tryout?"

New customers are the lifeblood of any business, but only if they stick around long enough to become old customers. A one-time buyer is welcome, but the ones who put money in the bank are those who come back again and again.

One breed of new customer that's tricky to develop is the neophyte, the guy or gal who is new to the world your business inhabits. Maybe they are a first-time home buyer or a young couple setting up a college fund for their newborn. The way you and your staff respond to that newbie can make or break your relationship with them. Treat them like an idiot the first time and you'll never see them again. Treat them right, and you'll create a customer for life.

It's tough, though. A newbie doesn't know what questions to ask. He doesn't know what's do-able and what violates the laws of physics and/or the local building code. She may have seen a TV show where some lucky stiff's family room went from wreck to magazine-spread-worthy in thirty minutes and expect you to do the same. What's worse, she's going to take up way more of your valuable time than this measly little job is worth.

Sueann Blackwell, who has operated Merrillville Restyling in Merrillville, Indiana, since 1989, says it's not unusual for a neophyte to spend two hours going through the options for an upholstering job when she first sees them. They have also been known to ask for the impossible, she says. "One customer wanted a 12 by 20-inch Buick logo embroidered on his dash, but that's too big for an embroidery machine."

Customer education takes time

Blackwell insists on spending as much time as it takes to educate the new customer before they make a decision. "I show them all the options available to them," she explains. "Suedes, vinyls, cloths, welt cords, top-stitching, insert selections, embroidery—even though they get totally confused." She feels it's important that the new customer not make a decision based on partial information. It's also essential that they don't leap before they've looked. She adds, "I always tell them to go home and think about it."

The next time a newbie walks through your door, put yourself in their shoes for a minute. Remember what it was like when you went onto the field for your very first Little League tryout? If you were like most of us, the experience was a little intimidating. Everyone else seemed to know exactly what they were doing, but you weren't sure. You wanted to make the team, but the single most important goal was to avoid making a fool of yourself.

That's what the newbie is feeling when he comes into your business for the first time. He or she may not admit it—and may try to bluff their way through—but they are nervous about sounding dumb when they talk to the experts in the field.

Your first job, then, is to make the customer comfortable. Don't draw attention to his ignorance by telling him it's all right to be stupid. Instead, listen to his ideas in a non-judgmental way and ask him questions about what he needs at a level he can understand. Try to avoid using terms the customer may not have heard before, or, if you have to, explain them without being condescending.

Blackwell gets around the terminology problem (and several others) by showing rather than telling. "I show them a lot of samples," she says. "It's a lot easier than trying to have them visualize it in their head. I also have a lot of pictures of our work with all the different options available."

What's a lifetime customer worth?

Consider a shop like Blackwell's. Most restyling customers are serial car owners. They don't just trick out one set of wheels and live with it; they buy, sell, trade, and do it all over again and again. Do the math on the customer who gets a different car every couple of years. If the shop's average job is $1,500 and the customer stays with them for twenty years, he'll bring ten jobs—or $15,000—through the door. If the gross margin (before overhead expenses) is 40%, the shop owner will put $6,000 in the bank.

Plug in your company's numbers and think about that the next time you're tempted to brush off a newbie.

One temptation to resist is the urge to make the customers' decisions for them. It's easy to limit the number of options you show them in the interests of time or from the mistaken belief that you're clarifying the issues for them. The problem, of course, is that later they may discover that you've done so and misunderstand your motivations. It's fine to guide them in their decision-making, but don't give them any reason to think you've shortchanged them.

Another thing to keep in mind with newbies is that praise goes a long way toward making them feel good about their decisions. Go back to Little League for a minute. Which coach got the most out of his team, the one who screamed at you about errors or the one who applauded when you did something right? The same is true for a new customer. As they make each incremental decision that goes into drawing up the specs for their order, confirm each decision as a good one. They'll feel better about themselves—and about doing business with you.

That's the goal, of course, to make the neophyte customer so comfortable with your business that he'll come back the next time he has an itch that needs to be scratched. Keep in mind that the second job will be easier to explain than the first one and the third one will be easier than the second, and so on. That makes the time and patience you spend on the newbie customer an investment, not an expense.

Chapter 9

Beat The Big Box

"Because you know your customers as people,
you better understand exactly what turns them on."

Independent retailers face more competition than ever before. On-line drop shippers are a known and growing problem. But one of the most persistent threats is from bricks-and-mortar stores in your own market—big box retailers whose volume purchasing, minimum-wage labor, and huge advertising budgets make them a force to be reckoned with regardless of what the small local business sells. You can beat the big box, though, if you play your own game and not theirs.

Cut-throat pricing is the biggest advantage the major chains have over the little guy. There's no escaping their ability to buy in volumes that get the best terms, thereby allowing them to undercut the independent substantially. They also don't generally pay their service people and installers much (if they have any), so their labor costs are lower, too.

You can't beat them at that game, so play to your own strengths instead. Price isn't the only reason a consumer chooses one place over another. Quality of service is just as important as price, especially when it comes to installing customer purchases in their homes or cars. Do your potential customers really want some minimum-wage-inspired mechanic learning how to cut up a headliner to drop in a sunroof by practicing on their car?

You, on the other hand, either do that work yourself or supervise a trained, experienced technician so your customer knows the job is going to be done right the first time. That should be worth a few dollars more.

Make your size work for your customers

Small size may actually be an advantage, too. The big store has to be a wide but shallow river—it carries a lot of different inventory but isn't very deep in any one line. As a specialist, though, you can become known for having everything the customer needs for one type of purchase (including the expertise to get it installed right). You don't have to worry about carrying faucets, lighting fixtures, and air conditioners, for example, if your shop is the kitchen cabinet design leader in the market.

The trick is finding a market segment the megastore can't serve very well. The ideal niche is one where one size does **not** fit all and where installation requires knowing more than just which end of the screwdriver to hold.

You also offer the customer something else the big box can't: a personal relationship. The next time your customer has the urge to remodel the family room, she can come back to the team that did the kitchen—yours. Your staff knows her, knows her house and family, and has built a level of trust that only a long-term relationship can inspire. Go back to the megastore and see if you can find the guy who did your last job. If it's been more than nine months, he's probably been replaced, along with the department head and even the store manager.

A solid niche market and good personal relationships with your customers give you another advantage over the big box. **You** can be very successful at selling add-ons to your current customers whereas the clerk in the megastore (if you can find one) is charged with doing little more than ringing up the sale and processing your credit card. For you, on the other hand, selling a new countertop to the customer who came in for cabinets should be an automatic. Plus, you can probably show the customer some price advantages of doing multiple jobs simultaneously.

Yes, your advertising can compete, too

Then there is the matter of advertising, where, believe it or not, you actually have an edge as well. You have a message about something other than price and you have the ability to target your promotion in ways the big guys can only drool over.

First the message. You know about the level of service you provide, the friendly personal touch, technical expertise, and dedication to quality you deliver. Does your potential customer know? He or she will if you reach out to them with some pro-active marketing that carries that message.

You can also tailor your message almost to the individual customer level, which is something a big box multi-department retailer can't do. Because you know your customers as people, you better understand exactly what turns them on, what bells and whistles appeal to them and which ones are repellent. You can use that knowledge to shape your promotion.

Chain retailer advertising—circulars full of specials, full page ads touting the deal of the day, TV spots in the Super Bowl—is hugely inefficient when it comes to reaching the one best customer for a specialized product. Advertising media like that work for the megastores because they build total store traffic, something you don't have to worry about.

You can run small-scale-big-impact campaigns with little or no waste if you pick and choose your media and venues based on your knowledge of your customers. When the only people who see your ads are those in the market for your product, the return on your advertising investment skyrockets. Ads in home show programs, signage at the shows, your logo on a builder's dream home, post cards sent to the local garden club's members—these are ways you can promote your business without breaking the bank.

Tired of battling the big guys? Just step back and count the ways you can compete. If you use your natural advantages, there are plenty of ways to beat the big box.

Chapter 10

Case Study:

Schweser's Little Stores On The Prairie

"In today's big-box world, the 125-year-old chain
of women's clothing stores has beaten the odds
by staying true to its roots."

It's hard to imagine a business facing more pitfalls than Schweser's Stores. The 125-year-old, fourth-generation company operates women's specialty stores in small Midwestern farm towns. Its markets grow at a glacial rate (if at all); its suppliers, with offices in New York and factories on the other side of the world, don't exactly have their fingers on the customer's pulse; and there is at least one Wal-Mart within a couple of miles of every one of Schweser's stores. Despite these obstacles, the company opened its 23rd and 24th stores in 2005.

Why have the descendants of founder George Schweser continued the business he established in 1880? And how have they managed to do it?

Ty Smith, the 32-year-old president of the company, answers the first question somewhat ingenuously. "It's a family business, and it's part of what the family is," he says. "There is a bit of an obligation to keeping it going."

The "how" question takes a little longer to answer. Keeping the $12 million (approximate annual sales) company going takes deep customer knowledge, a willingness to change and, above all, frugality. The trick to profitability in these conditions, says Ty, is, "You have to do what you have to do to stay alive."

A near-genetic thriftiness runs through the company's history. George Schweser, Ty's great-grandfather, walked more than 100 miles from the railroad station rather than rent a horse and buggy to reach David City, Neb., where he purchased the first store with a partner for $700.

At the turn of the century, founder George's four sons worked in the general store when they weren't in school. During one particularly busy holiday season, George started to fill a sack with peanuts for a customer only to discover that the boys had been snacking while they worked and the peanut barrel was full of empty shells. George got even several years later when his oldest son, Harold, graduated from Northwestern University and came home to apply his business degree to the family business. George took his newly educated son to the grocery department and assigned him to begin taking inventory. The first task: Count the peanuts in the barrel.

During the Depression, George's son, Fred, ordered the company's buyers to purchase only "needles and pins" in an effort to limit their spending, an expression Fred's daughter, Barbara Schweser Smith, says is still heard in the company offices. "We try to undersell the competition," says Barbara, who is Ty's mother. "From a marketing standpoint, we have to be in the market every week looking for deals."

"We run a pretty tight ship," Ty explains. "We don't have a whole lot of overhead. That's been one of our keys—not to overgrow our size and keep the costs low."

The need to keep costs low is one major reason Schweser's stores are located only in small towns. Half of the 24 apparel specialty stores are in Nebraska, with the rest in South Dakota, Minnesota, Iowa, Missouri and Kansas, all within a day's drive of company headquarters in Fremont, Neb. The average population of those towns is just over 20,000, or about the same number of people as work in New York's Empire State Building. Only two of Schweser's stores are in towns larger than 30,000 people. The largest city with a Schweser's store is St. Joseph, Mo., population 73,990; the smallest is Atlantic, Iowa, with 7,257.

Schweser's small-town survival guide

Conventional wisdom holds that small towns like these are dead or dying, but a closer examination reveals that Schweser's location strategy has actually put the chain in some pretty solid markets. As Jim Otto, president of the Nebraska Retail Federation, points out, "Towns under 5,000 people are the ones that are actually shrinking. The towns like Grand Island, Kearney, Columbus and North Platte, they're all growing. People are moving to job centers. The small towns that are shrinking aren't the retail centers." The towns where Schweser's operates grew slightly as a group (0.4% in total) from 2000 to 2004, according to the U.S. Census Bureau. Not Las Vegas, exactly, but growing areas nonetheless.

"You can't believe everything you read," Ty says. "If there was nothing here, nobody would live here. Most of the towns we're in are agriculture-based, and agriculture, believe it or not, is still a major part of the American economy. There are still a lot of farmers out here, and they still have wives who like to shop."

"The farmer that used to have a truck that held 300 bushels now has a semi that holds 1,000 bushels," Otto explains. "Instead of going to the local town, he just keeps on rolling to the larger terminal elevator. That's why those little towns are dwindling, but the larger towns are actually growing." He says farm women drive to shop, too: "Some towns draw from a hundred-mile radius because of where they are. For example, North Platte probably draws from 90 miles north."

Of course, Scheweser's isn't the only retailer that figured out there's a market out there on the prairies. Sam Walton founded an empire on stores in places just like Fremont, Neb. Today, JC Penney, Younkers, Wal-Mart, K-Mart and Target compete on Main Street, as do apparel chains like Herbergers, Gordmans and Christopher & Banks, among many others. Staying profitable in the face of that kind of competition requires constant attention to cost, expenses and customers.

"We only open stores if we can find somebody who has a location who is willing to work with us on an affordable lease," Ty explains. "Generally, we like to move into spots where another clothing store had been, so we don't have to build the dressing rooms. Ideally, we'd just move in without spending a lot of money building a brand-new store." Two-thirds of the stores are in enclosed malls, but there are several in downtown and strip mall locations as well. Most are 5,000 square feet or smaller, although some of the older downtown locations, originally department stores, are twice that size.

Corporate overhead is low, too. There are a grand total of six employees in the corporate offices in Fremont and a scant dozen at the 10,000-square-foot distribution center. Ty's sister, Betsy Smith Hocking, 35, handles almost all the buying from her home office in Philadelphia, Pa. Most stores operate with just six or seven employees.

Price, value, and service

Low expenses are only part of the equation. Perhaps the tougher task is balancing customer demand for low prices with the fickle nature of the fashion business. That begins by precisely defining the market, which Schweser's has done, according to Ty. "Our customers are women over the age of 30," he says. "We don't target the teenagers and the 20-somethings."

Schweser's customers are concerned about looking good, just like their sisters on Fifth Avenue or Rodeo Drive. "Our customer wants a lot of value," says Betsy, who travels to New York's fashion district by train at least once a week to keep the stores stocked with merchandise. The customer "wants to be in style, but does not want to stand out," Betsy explains. "Schweser's shoppers read magazines and watch TV, so they know what the looks are, although they may not be willing to fully embrace them."

"It's a more conservative look than what you'd find at stores on the coasts, or even what you'd find at the other stores in the malls that cater to a younger customer," Ty adds. "The colors have to be right. The styles have to be right. We have to be fashion aware, but we don't have to be on the cutting edge."

Price means a lot to Schweser's customers, according to Betsy. "The towns just don't have much money," she notes. "The people here are struggling to make ends meet, so our customer base cannot afford to go on weekend shopping binges."

And there is always the competition. "We want to make sure we're providing better value than they are," Ty says. "We're not a discount store, but we're certainly a high-value store." The chain stays at the lower end of the price point, an approach that fits very well into its customers' lifestyle.

"From the small-town merchant's perspective right now," Otto observes, "the real challenge is figuring out a niche so they can coexist with the big-box stores. Small-town businesspeople concentrate on service and their customers' likes and dislikes."

After 125 years of serving small-town women in the upper Midwest, Schweser's knows its customer and the value of service. Company controller Helen Lanin, a 52-year employee, says doing business in places like Huron, S.D., has its marketing advantages: "In small towns, you know everybody," she says. "When you walk through the door, the manager calls you by name. That's very important."

"Since we have an older customer base, many people come in and really need help," Betsy explains. "They need help finding the clothing; making sure it matches. There are sales associates who call customers when things come in that they know they would like. They really know their customer base."

"We know if we give up the service, which is kind of unique, it will never work," observes Barbara. "We have a lot of older customers, and their style is to come in and let us put it together for them. But they want the same price—or better—than they would get from the big-box stores."

"We take a really, really personal interest in it. It's our life," Betsy says. "It's what we've known, so it's part of every aspect of our life."

Changing with the times

It's a constant struggle to beat the competition, but it's one the company has fought and won before. One reason has been its chameleon-like ability to change as circumstances warrant. Each of the first three generations reinvented the business. George Schweser opened a general store with barrels of peanuts and bolts of fabric. His son, Fred, turned it into a group of small-town department stores offering clothing for the entire family as well as draperies and home accessories.

Ty's mother, Barbara, the third generation to manage the company, changed direction entirely. She dropped departments like home furnishings and bridal wear and refined the concept into small specialty stores offering value-priced women's fashions. She joined the company when it was in financial difficulty and ran it from 1973 to 2003, growing it from seven to 22 stores in the process. "I changed it a lot," she recalls. "I actually remade it at different points."

Over the years, Barbara didn't hesitate to try different formats. She experimented with discount stores, junior fashions and shops catering to full-figured women. Large cities weren't entirely out of bounds, either, although stores in Omaha and Lincoln, Neb., proved to not fit the company cost structure.

The current approach may have worked best in recent years, but there's nothing sacred about it, according to Betsy. Are there other formats in future? "Not right now, but there could be," she says. "We had others in the past. You never say never."

Ty, who joined the company as president in 2003, "has a vision now, just as I did," Barbara says proudly. "I reinvented it during my 30 years, and he's doing the same thing."

"As far as strategic planning goes, it's a very informal process here," Ty notes. "There isn't a lot of time or energy or resources available to just sit down and think about what are the next ten steps. We have a plan, but for the most part, it's in our heads."

Ty says he isn't in any hurry to change. "We feel like we know the ladies in the small towns," he asserts. "That's our customer, and that's who we know. That's how we do business."

Ty acknowledges that the company still needs to grow sales. The way to do that, he says, is by adding locations. "It's a big challenge to get comparable store growth within these towns that are maybe not growing in size and their economies aren't growing," he concedes. "But certainly there are other towns out there that have good opportunities within them." He recognizes that "given our current ways of doing things, there is probably a limit," he says. "We can't drive trucks to Oklahoma. But when we reach that limit, I'm sure we'll find another way of doing things."

One thing not likely to change in the near future, Ty says, is family ownership of the company. "I can't imagine a scenario where it's not a family business," he says. "We're not such a high-growth business that we would need any huge infusion of capital or outsiders to take positions in the company." But it would be a long time before a fifth generation is ready to take over, since Ty, recently married, currently has no children. Sister Betsy has three children, but the oldest is only six.

"Ty is young, and he is enjoying it," Betsy observes. As for her own future in her position, she adds, "I'll definitely keep doing it for a while."

Originally published in *Family Business*, www.familybusinessmagazine.com

Chapter 11
The Magic of Pricing

"Setting prices is part art and part science
with maybe a little management magic
thrown in for good measure."

When it comes to prices in your business, how much is enough and how much is too much? How do you set your prices? Buy low and sell high is the obvious answer, but for many companies, especially those with a mixture of retail merchandise and services, bricks-and-mortar and online competition, and customers driven one day by a penny-pinching budget and the next by the lust called gotta-have-whatever-at-any-price, there aren't any easy answers.

Setting prices requires that even the most experienced manager or owner take a few moments every once in a while to dust off the calculator, get the accountant on the phone, and do some serious figuring. It's tempting to just mark all merchandise up by a fixed percentage and figure labor at a flat rate comparable to what your competitors charge, but that's not managing for profit, it's hoping for one. There are several factors that you should consider.

Start with the cost of goods sold. That's the amount you pay the manufacturer, wholesaler, or whomever for the merchandise you sell, whether at retail or as part of a service job. But it also includes the cost of acquiring those goods (shipping and handling), carrying them in inventory (interest expense), and allowances for returns and defective merchandise. If you pay any salespeople a commission or spiff, that needs to be taken into account, too.

For service work, you have to cover your direct labor costs on each job. These include not only an appropriate portion of your technicians' annual salaries, but also their benefits, payroll taxes, unemployment insurance, worker's compensation insurance, etc.

What about the cost of your time? Whether you are a one-person business or simply provide indirect supervision of your staff, your time is a cost that has to be covered. One way to approach this is to divide what you expect to personally earn on an annual basis (including those items above but not your profit from the business—I'll talk about that later) by 2,000, which is roughly the number of working hours during the year. Let's say your "salary" plus benefits is $100,000. Your hourly labor cost is $50. Multiply that number by the hours you estimate you'll personally spend on the job, add in the other worker's costs, and you have your direct labor costs.

Just to make sure you've covered all your costs, here's a brief checklist:

Cost of Goods Sold	Overhead
Wholesale price	Rent
Shipping	Utilities
Carrying cost	Taxes
Returns	Insurance
Sales commissions	Facilities Maintenance
Labor Costs	Fixed Asset Depreciation
Wages	Professional Fees
Benefits	Dues & Subscriptions
Payroll Taxes	Telephone
Unemployment Insurance	Office Supplies
Workman's Compensation	Office Salaries & Benefits
	Owner's Salary & Benefits

Your markup

Once you know how much the merchandise or job costs, you mark it up to provide a profit. One way is to use what's known as "keystone" pricing, which simply means doubling the cost to arrive at the selling price. This provides a 50% gross profit margin. That's why retailers can put goods on sale for 40% off and still make a profit. It works fine, but it isn't always the best choice.

You can also use manufacturers' suggested retail pricing, which even further simplifies the calculations. Nationally uniform prices, of course don't reflect local market conditions, much less the individual business owner's costs of doing business. Remember, too, that they're designed to help the manufacturer move more merchandise, not necessarily help you make more money.

Using a standard markup sounds simple, but that's really only the beginning of sound pricing strategy. You also have to be sure that the gross profit is large enough to cover your overhead, or the indirect costs of operating your business, and still leave a net profit. Whether you're marking up merchandise or deciding on a labor rate, you've got to build in something to cover the rent—and all those other bills you pay every month.

Every business has indirect expenses (not related to the cost of a piece of merchandise or a particular employee's labor on a job) that have to be paid. The obvious ones include your building and what it costs to operate it (utilities, maintenance, taxes, insurance), your fixtures, tools, office equipment, vehicles and other fixed assets (their cost on an annual basis is your depreciation expense), your salary and benefits (especially health insurance), not to mention the office manager and other general employees. Don't forget to add in your property and casualty and liability insurance premiums, accountant's fees, advertising and marketing expenses, office supplies, telephone, and so on and so on. While you're at it, make sure you include an annual contribution to your own retirement plan, be it a 401-K, SEP-IRA, or whatever.

Finally, add something for net profit. That's the whole point of running the business, right? The net profit, by the way, is not the same as your salary as the manager or owner. Your salary is payment for your labor managing the business. If you're the owner, the net profit is the return on your investment and the compensation your receive for the risks you take. There's a big difference.

The total dollar amount of your shop's gross profit, the figure that has to be larger than your overhead expense, is also dependent on how much merchandise you sell or how many jobs you complete. These are determined, at least in part, by the prices you charge. If your prices are too high, customers will run away, so it can be a vicious circle. Cost-based pricing is all well and good, but ultimately, the prices you charge are determined by what your customers are willing to pay. That's where a whole raft of other factors comes into play.

Pricing against the competition

How much is the competition charging? Brick-and-mortar retailers are bedeviled by online shops that have minimal overhead. Some of them never even take title to the merchandise they sell, much less provide for returns in the case of defects or mistakes. Other companies, like well-run, sophisticated garages, for example, are plagued by shade-tree mechanics who have never even seen an insurance agent, much less bought a policy. There are some customers who are going to do business with those folks because price is what drives their decision-making, whether by choice or necessity. Quite frankly, you can't let those customers set your prices because you'll never be able to compete—price-wise—with the no-overhead operators.

Your answer has to be providing value to your customers that justifies the higher prices you charge. You provide value by standing behind the merchandise you sell with reasonable return policies, providing side-by-side hands-on comparisons of optional equipment, and helping the customer make intelligent choices with face-to-face advice from knowledgeable personnel. These are all things the online drop-shipper has trouble doing. These may be intangibles that are difficult to quantify, but they add value to the customer's transaction with your business, making higher prices easier for them to swallow.

This same value-plus strategy holds when you're competing with a large chain store. They can't match the personal service and relationship with each individual customer provided by a small shop owner. Their volume purchasing may enable them to offer lower prices, but they'll never know every customer by name and every customer's favorite flavor of ice cream.

Competitive labor rates are tricky. Again, you're probably wise to not compete on price with the weekend handyman or shade tree mechanic. Instead, count on the value you deliver to justify a higher price. Your installers and technicians are fairly paid and receive at least some benefits, so they'll be around when the customer comes back. If they've moved on, you'll have hired someone else to take their place. You'll also have trained those staff members and added your own expertise to help them over the rough spots. Your customer should have a sense that his job is being handled by a team or professionals, which makes it worth a higher price.

With all these factors to consider, setting prices is part art and part science with maybe a little management magic thrown in for good measure. To create a profit for your shop's pricing structure, take one part cost of goods sold, add a portion of labor, two scoops of overhead and a dose of competition, then stir rapidly with a sharp pencil.

Chapter 12

Specialty Market Case Study:

Artists And Their Prices

"There may be a price so high the customer won't pay it,
but patrons seldom buy a piece of art just because it's cheap."

"Craft is undervalued," declares Chicago gallery owner Peter Vale. Consequently, many artists struggle to make a living, as do many gallery owners. Few would disagree with his assessment of the problem, but unanimity about a solution is harder to come by.

The one thing both artists and their galleries agree on, though, is that pricing is an important issue that begins with how much the artists can charge for their work. Ron Wilcocks says, "We are 100% supportive of the prices our artists set." Wilcocks owns Earthwood Artisans and Earthwood Collections in Estes Park, Colorado, with his wife Ann.

How should an artist set prices? "There are so many aspects to that question," answers Montrose, Colorado artist Nick Zappa, who has been making and selling stoneware pottery with his wife Joan for thirty years. "We try to get a price for our work that is reasonable for not only us but for the store owner as well," he adds. "They need to be able to sell it and make a decent profit and we need to make a decent profit."

That's a worthwhile sentiment, but the first question that comes to mind is what is a "decent" profit? Profit, of course, is simply the difference between the cost of an item and the price at which it is sold. For a craft artist, costs include direct items like materials and labor as well as overhead expenses like fuel, studio rent, and insurance. Aside from setting a minimum, these factors have nothing to do with what an artist should charge.

What about the aesthetic value of a piece? What about the years of experience the artist has applied to producing an object of delight? What role does free market economics play? Veteran jewelry maker Nancy Daniels Hubert says, "I don't go by materials and things like that. The less I want to part with a piece, the higher I charge."

Customers set prices

Ultimately, the retail customer determines the price an artist can charge. Rather than start with what it costs to make a piece, the artist should look at what similar work is selling for in galleries around the country and work backwards, taking into account that most retailers use a keystone markup, which produces a gross profit margin of fifty percent of the retail price. The markup isn't simply double the artist's price, though, because there are other cost factors involved, particularly shipping. "We have to figure out our pricing depending on what it costs us to get the item in our store," says Steve Fishman, who operates Stowe Craft Gallery in Stowe, Vermont.

Some gallery owners go beyond the keystone benchmark, however, which says something about whether prices in general are as high as the market will bear. Art is not a commodity, so there is little elasticity of demand in the marketplace. In other words, there may be a price so high the customer won't pay it, but patrons seldom buy a piece of art just because it's cheap.

There is also a big psychological aspect to prices, according to Vale, who operates the shop carrying his name in the heart of the River North gallery district in Chicago. "We have a range of customers from big-time collectors to the general public, and sometimes, the collectors think something isn't good enough if it's priced too low," Vale points out.

Wilcocks agrees. They carry work from about 230 artists in their two galleries, and he says, "We've had to counsel artists in regard to underpricing themselves. Some of it comes from emerging artists who are a little timid. They're eager to please, so they hesitate to name what they consider a big price."

"You need to know what the market is" for your work, recommends glass artist Tom Fuhrman. "Do some prototypes and do some test marketing." Fuhrman, whose studio is in Woodbury, Tennessee, says, "People don't really know a lot about their markets. We're in a business that's pretty unsophisticated."

Consistency counts

According to every artist and gallery owner I talked to, another important factor is consistency of price from one distribution channel to another. "Lately, we're becoming more sensitive to the issue of the internet and artists who sell direct," Fishman says. "We always ask. It affects whether we want to do business with an artist. For us, it's not a question of whether they sell directly to the public, it's just, is their pricing going to be similar to ours?"

Vale adds another facet to that issue: "It's really important for artists to be consistent if they're showing similar work from one gallery to the next." Hubert even goes a step further to protect the galleries who carry her work by generally not exhibiting at shows in the towns where they're located.

Setting prices isn't something many artists feel particularly comfortable doing, but it's an essential skill to develop if they hope to have successful long-term careers. "The sad thing is, we're not just artists anymore," Fuhrman observes. "It's more about marketing. It's more about running a business. It sure as hell isn't much fun, but that's what you've got to put up with."

Chapter 13

Two Ways To Compete Without Chopping Prices

"As long as we're promoting quality
and being fair about pricing,
I don't worry too much about our competitors."

Price-cutting competitors are like rust on a steel tool: as soon as you clean it off, it starts forming again. As soon as one cheap competitor goes out of business, another one takes his place. And, just like insidious oxidation, price-cutters can't be ignored. If you don't pay attention, they'll erode your company's business.

One way to respond to price competition is to meet or beat it at the lowball game. Unfortunately, there always seems to be somebody willing to go even lower and your bottom line suffers as a result. Admittedly, depending on your company's finances, that may be the only way to go. But there are alternative strategies that can allow you to build your business even if you're not the cheapest shop in town.

One way is to diversify so that you can afford to pass up a job or two without worrying about its impact on your bottom line. Pete Bennett, owner of CoachCraft, Inc., in Lexington, Kentucky, provides as many automotive restyling services as he can think of in a successful effort to build revenue and fully use his shop's capacity. He bought the business in 1991, the third owner since its founding in 1953. He believes it is the largest shop in Lexington, but doesn't let market position blind him to the impact of competition.

"You get some guys working out of their garages, no insurance, no license fees, no workman's comp, buying parts COD. Their biggest expense is their yellow pages ad," he says. "I'd be foolish to not pay attention to them." On the other hand, he adds, "As long as we're promoting quality and being fair about pricing, I don't worry too much about our competitors."

CoachCraft sells and installs everything from headliners to carpets, with specialists to design and produce custom upholstery and seat covers as well as complete leather interiors. They also install lumbar support systems, heated seats, wood-grain dashes, sun roofs, and convertible tops from the hydraulics to the frame and canvas. Truck bed liners and covers are naturals for the shop. Repair and restoration is a big part of the business, too.

Volume can't trump quality

Volume is important, but not at the expense of quality, according to Bennett, who believes better work supports higher prices. "The quality speaks for itself, "he says. "For example, when we install a sunroof, we do a one-piece headliner instead of a two-piece. Ours looks more professional and less like an aftermarket product."

By offering a wide variety of related products and services, Bennett avoids some of the vagaries of the marketplace. If one thing goes out of style—if Paris Hilton's dog jumps out of her car's moonroof and the openings become unfashionable next year, for example—his total sales won't be hit too hard. Conversely, if a product category gets hot, Bennett probably already has the inventory and technicians in place to handle it, giving him a good jump on the competitor who has to track down suppliers or learn a new technique to respond to the demand. He's also able to cross-sell customers, adding profitable volume to many jobs and building repeat retail business, which is difficult if you only sell one product.

Bennett's diversity strategy goes a step beyond many shops'. While 90% of his work is on cars and trucks, he also does a fair amount for boat owners. In addition, CoachCraft takes on commercial upholstery jobs for restaurants and other businesses. He also bids on jobs for the nearby University of Kentucky, especially the athletic department. It's all about fully utilizing the shop's capacity so that desperate measures—like cutting prices to stay afloat—aren't necessary.

Bennett not only tries to attract many different types of work, he also maintains a balance between retail customers and dealer subcontracts. He estimates that his business is split just about equally between the two. Retail jobs generate a higher profit margin, of course, but the dealer business provides volume to maintain capacity utilization. Because he has both, Bennett can afford to maintain his prices, even to dealers. "Dealers who come to us for restyling--sunroofs and leather kits—are pretty price conscious," he says. "They play us off against the competition. We walk away from a lot of business. If it's a package deal, a sunroof and a leather kit combo, I may give them a little bit of a break."

He takes a similarly firm stand with retail customers who bring in their own aftermarket trim covers or reproductions: "Some people buy the products online and beg us to put it on. I tell them I'm missing the opportunity to make a few dollars of profit on the parts, so I'm going to have to mark my labor up. They usually go along with that, especially when they figure out they can't install it themselves."

Doing one thing very, very well

Lee Muntean, owner of AAA Convertible & Sun Roofs in Costa Mesa, California, has adopted exactly the opposite strategy for beating the competition. He targets a niche market and does one thing—but he does it very, very well. Muntean specializes in convertible tops for high-end foreign cars, a niche he finds easy to defend because the quality demands are so high. "There are a lot of people who can put a canvas top on, but they can't deal with the fine work, especially the mechanicals," he observes. "With a Porsche, just like adjusting braces on your teeth, you have to adjust the framework periodically for thirty days. Your average trim shop can't do that for the price they charge."

Muntean's shop, basically a one-man operation, has been open for ten years. He briefly staffed up to take a standard approach offering to do just about any kind of work and sell a variety of restyling accessory lines, but decided that he would make more money specializing in a niche market. Now, his reputation for quality work keeps him plenty busy.

It also provides a strong floor under his prices. "If customers don't want to pay for quality, I don't bother. They can go someplace else," Muntean says with confidence.

Like Bennett, Muntean handles both retail and subcontract customers. His pricing for dealers and general repair shops isn't driven by a need to beat the competition, but there is another factor he takes into account: the dealer's margin. When it comes to pricing work subcontracted to him by body shops and garages, he's careful to allow them to make a profit without undercutting his retail price. "One thing I don't want them to do is give the jobs away. That hurts me." In the ideal situation, the garage's customer would pay the same if he came directly to Muntean and vice versa.

Any business owner or manager will tell you there is always somebody willing to undercut your price. One way to respond is to make a knee-jerk price cut of your own. As these two successful business owners demonstrate, though, that's not necessarily the only way to build your business.

Chapter 14
Specialty Market Case Study:
Sportswear And Speedwear

"Making a profit in the rag trade isn't automatic."

Most automotive speed shops don't look much like a Brooks Brothers store or The Gap, but a surprisingly large number of them are in the apparel business just the same. Some keep it simple, with a few caps and a line of shop-logo t-shirts for sale, while others devote significant floor space to everything from racing suits and protective underwear to team jackets and big-ticket eyewear. The question is, should you?

Mark Bogucki, Marketing Manager for performance parts wholesaler VSI-HP, sees opportunities in apparel sales: "There is a big want for all that," he says. "You go to any drag race, you see your top eliminator guys and sport racers into apparel. The same thing with your local stock car tracks, they all have their apparel. Mom, dad, even the kids. It's a family thing. Everybody down to the children are all decked out in the same colors. It is a big thing right now."

One point to keep in mind is that there are basically two kinds of apparel sold in automotive speed shops: performance wear and street wear. The first category includes technical products worn at the track by drivers and crew members while the second is pretty much everything else. Business considerations such as markups, competition, and inventory turnover apply equally, however, and either or both may have a place in your showroom.

One indicator of the potential in the performance market is the entry of a relatively new competitor—at least in motor sports apparel. It's Oakley Sports Marketing, a company known internationally for its high-style, high-demand sunglasses and well as high-tech gear for numerous other sports. Oakley Motor Sports Marketing Manager Todd Hayes explains that their entry into the motor sports market came about through work it did with the military using the fabric Carbon-X™. "We integrated that material into some race boots and that was our first product for the market. That has now turned into a glove and into base layer underwear," he says.

Impulse buyers

Hayes points out that capitalizing on customer emotions is one of the major reasons a speed shop owner should carry at least some apparel: "A lot of times, a new pair of gloves or boots is an impulse buy. It's not something you always need, but if it's cool and new, you want to buy it."

Lou Lobsinger, owner of Detroit Muscle Authentic Speedwear, draws attention to another, similar, customer reaction. "It's a lot of fun for people to buy apparel," he says. "Manifolds aren't necessarily a lot of fun to shop for. A cool, new collectible t-shirt, that's fun. People love to buy apparel."

Detroit Muscle is primarily in the street wear business, where fashion rules. Their emphasis is on style and visual appeal, with a great deal of thought going into the logo and product appearance as well as its construction. The products are true collectibles, with a limited run of each model produced each year. Their line includes everything from ball caps and beanies to t-shirts, work shirts, and Zippo lighters.

Healthy margins

Fun is one thing, but what about profit? How does a jobber make money on a small-ticket item like a t-shirt or a cap? "We offer a $500 planogram with a retail price of about $1200," Lobsinger explains. "Those are good margins on good products you can sell all day long." The selection doesn't take up much floor space, either, with a full selection of merchandise in an easy-to-assemble rack with a three-by-three-foot footprint. Merchandising includes signage, stickers, posters, and banners. "It's really a plug-and-play kind of operation," he adds.

Hayes agrees on the profit potential, saying the performance retailer should look at it as "an opportunity to make fifty points on a product." He adds that retailers with a vision can "go to a team and say, 'I'm a one-stop-shop for all your needs: packs, traveling bags, T-shirts, hats, jackets, sweatshirts, we've got it all.' But the retailer has to invest in the forecast." One big reason Oakley is pushing into motor sports is the opportunity to cross-sell eyewear, jackets, and other merchandise.

Making a profit in the rag trade (as the apparel business is known on New York's Seventh Avenue) isn't automatic, of course. The speed shop owner who complains about online discounters of performance parts isn't going to be any happier with the number of places on the web competing for the apparel customer. There are also thousands of local embroidery shops and screen printers eager to put race team logos on anything from headbands to socks.

High-profile promotion

Retailers who work with companies like Oakley and Detroit Muscle, though, can depend on a high degree of price protection and investment in brand promotion to maintain margins. Hayes points out, "We rely on our relationships and our athlete lists to expose the product and get media coverage. What's better than Jamie McMurray or Kasey Kahne getting out of a car wearing your product and speaking about it? You can't pay for advertising like that." For the retailer, Hayes says, "It's a trickle-down effect. You spread that message to the Saturday night guy and the club guy."

Fashion is fickle though, whether you're Tommy Hilfiger or Tom the tune-up guy, which means you have to be on top of your inventory. "One thing you've got to keep in mind when you get into apparel is that you've got to keep the mix fresh," Lobsinger warns. "You've got to keep changing the stuff. It's got to be hot and it's got to be new. When the customers start to see the coverage the shirts get in magazines and they see their heroes wearing them, you've got to have them in stock."

He also points out that the merchandise doesn't have an indefinite shelf life like an air filter. "Most white shirts that sit on the shelf for two weeks, if they get a little sun, become yellow shirts," he says.

Even with these caveats, adding an apparel line to your shop's marketing mix may make sense for you. Whether you choose technical performance products, snazzy street wear, or a combination of both, you don't have to bet the ranch on your initial investment and, as Lobsinger says, "You're talking about strong profit margins and very, very low return rates. In terms of per-square-footage sales, it makes sense."

Chapter 15

Marketing in Cyberspace: Not A Buck Rogers Idea

"The website is essentially another complete business location."

"You can do anything on the web, but it's got to pay," says Mike Stutland, owner of Artique Galleries in Lexington, Kentucky. His observation sums up the quandary of business owners considering how much—if any—time and money they should devote to marketing online.

The Internet offers many exciting business growth possibilities. You can have a simple website promoting your company or an online catalog offering thousands of items for mail-order purchase. You can email a personal note with a picture of a new product to an individual customer or send a newsletter highlighting new merchandise lines, upcoming events, and market trends to your entire database of customers. You can hold an auction, show portfolios from new suppliers, or list your business among the major tourist destinations in your area. The marketing possibilities are limited only by your imagination.

And your pocketbook. And manpower. And patience.

Customer Interaction

Art and craft galleries have been marketing online for many years. Stutland put his galleries online in 1999 and says, "The customer reaction has been mixed. Most of the orders that come through the Internet have taken further human interaction." He describes the process like this: "A lot of people find us on the Internet, contact us via email, then we move to the telephone and conduct our business that way."

Those customers may well not have been reached otherwise, however, so they represent new sales, according to Stutland. "The web site has attracted customers from beyond our normal market area," he says. "It has brought people into our stores, especially through our links with many tourist information sites." A feature on his site allows the potential customer to request driving directions and a road map to the galleries from just about anywhere in the United States.

Jan Pessin, manager of Freehand Fine Crafts in Los Angeles, says interactions with customers from their website work much the same way. "You can go to our website and, if we happen to have the item shown, you can contact us and we'll send it to you. If we don't have the exact item shown, but we have something different by that artist or something in the same vein, I can take a digital picture and send it to you." It's not fully-automated e-commerce, but it works.

Major Commitment

At the other end of the spectrum is the extensive web presence maintained by NJM Gallery, Portsmouth, NH. Owners Lois and Lee Kupersmith have considerable experience selling in cyberspace. "We've been online since early 1995," Lee Kupersmith says. "We were the first gallery online of any type."

NJM's website has over 300 pages and features thousands of pieces of museum-quality contemporary art glass blown by more than 100 artists. Customers can order online through a secure server, get toll-free live telephone support, and track their shipments through UPS. The website is essentially another complete business location—which happens to draw customers and artists from around the world who shop with their keyboard, mouse, and credit card.

The images the customer sees on the web are color-corrected pictures of the actual piece offered—not a sample. As Lee Kupersmith explains, "We show actual inventory, we don't just show samples, so we make sure our images look like the pieces. We take care to make sure the website is done so that we'd be happy buying a piece off of it ourselves." Maintaining a website like this is a full-time job. "It is a huge amount of work keeping a website up to date," according to Lee. "We update our site every day to keep a current inventory."

"Anything that's worthwhile takes time and effort," Lois Kupersmith adds. How worthwhile is it?

"I won't give out any numbers," says Lee, who devotes almost all of his time to the site while Lois runs the physical gallery, "but obviously we wouldn't be doing it if it weren't paying off."

Everybody's Doing It

The Kupersmiths aren't alone in finding cyberspace a profitable place to do business. Enter the exact phrase "art & craft gallery" into Google, and you'll see thousands of listings from around the world. Not all of these are galleries, but the search results are indicative of the growing use of online media to promote and sell fine arts and crafts.

"I think we have to be there (on the web) because it's not going to go away," Stutland says. "There will be more and more ways of using it and the group of people that use it is expanding."

The Pew Research Center, which tracks Internet and other media usage, says nearly 60% of American adults use the web for entertainment, email, keeping up with the news, and shopping. While there are some regional variations (the South dips below 50% while both coasts approach

70% usage), it's interesting to note that these figures are comparable to daily adult newspaper readership in the top fifty markets as reported by the Newspaper Advertising Association, which was 55% in 2002. One of the most attention-getting numbers in the Pew report is the high percentage of Internet users who have made a purchase online—45%! That's a lot of customers.

Tips From The Pros

In an exclusive interview, Chairman/CEO Chuck Curtis of Valentine Radford Advertising in Kansas City, Mo., interpreted for us the results of the agency's survey of 1000 online shoppers.

1. 89% of Internet shoppers use the Internet for product information. Make sure your web site is rich in product details.

2. 45% of Internet shoppers click on their local newspaper and 32% click on their local television station site. This is good news for businesses who can inexpensively buy advertising just on the local media's web site.

3. Also buy advertising in the email news updates that local news media send out. About half of online shoppers have signed up for these.

4. 58% of these shoppers have signed up for an online loyalty program. It's a smart idea to reward your best customers with a frequent buyer plan (like the frequent flier programs run by the airlines.) For example: Get a 10% discount on your next purchase when you spend $50.

5. More than a third of the survey (38%) use a wish list feature on the site for their purchases. These are items they would like to buy, but can't purchase at the moment, and they register their desires online.

6. About two-thirds of the time a shopper will research a product online and then buy it in the store.

7. Many retailers will publish their coupons for in-store use online because the distribution costs are so much lower than putting them in the newspaper or on direct mail.

8. Between 40% and 60% of shoppers (depending upon the amount they spend) strongly object to shipping charges. Many retailers build the price of these into the products, or offer free shipping above a certain amount; e.g., "Free shipping when you spend $50 or more."

9. 81% of shoppers expect to find a wider selection of products online. Remember that your market online is worldwide. If you find items that you can't display in your store because of limited retail space, put them on your web site.

Online Alternatives

Gallery-owned websites aren't the only way to the use the marketing potential of the web. There are several online craft "malls" where both galleries and artists market in groups. Many gallery owners with and without websites combine the convenience of digital photography with the ease of email to market pieces to receptive customers. Auction site e-Bay, often mistakenly thought of as only a venue for consumers to sell the gleanings from their attics, is also the on-line home to some hundreds of stores selling crafts and craft-related items as well as several hundred more art galleries.

Every gallery owner we talked to pointed out the amount of work involved, however, which is no small consideration. Sometimes, too, a little online imagination helps. Betsy Hills-Bush, owner of Drosselmeiers.com in Scarsdale, NY, says she once received a multi-tiered candle pyramid that had been crushed in shipment from the artist. She says, "I sold it in shards as a craft project on e-Bay."

Chapter 16

Blogging, Social Media, and Other Online Marketing

"If putting your business into cyberspace

has seemed like more trouble than it's worth,

maybe now is the time to reconsider your decision."

Did you know that more Americans use the Internet than read a newspaper every day? That's bad news for publishers, but great news for business owners and managers looking for ways to reach customers.

If you're like most business operators when you think of the Internet, you visualize a website for your company—and plenty of them have been built at considerable cost and effort. Many business websites are e-commerce equipped, loaded with pictures and long lists of links to related sites, and other useful (and expensive) features. But there are other ways to use the ever-evolving online medium that can be just as (if not more) effective—and cost a whole lot less.

One way to market in cyberspace is with a blog, a type of web presence that has many interesting possibilities. A blog can be nothing more than a simple collection of written entries about anything (or nothing) that's posted on the web for the curious to read. Literally millions of them exist and more are coming online every day because they're cheap (often free!) and very, very easy to create. But how do you use a blog to market your business? By making it the centerpiece of an online community of your customers and potential customers.

Another approach is to sign up for Facebook or MySpace or one of the other rapidly-proliferating social networks. While there are some major differences between blogging and marketing through social networks, many of the same principles apply.

The main feature of both is a sort of message board where you make diary-like entries about topics of interest. In the case of a specialty shop owner, that could be the local hobby scene, events where your customers have competed, developments in technology, new product reviews, or similar subjects. The entries don't have to be long or even particularly literate just as long as they're about subjects you think your customers care about.

The biggest added feature of a social network page is your ability to reach customers (and potential customers) who have signed up to "friend" you. With luck, they'll keep their connection to you and see your messages every time they visit their own social site page.

What makes either one a "community" is your customers' ability to post their own messages along with yours, either in response to the ones you've posted or about subjects that they'd like to discuss. In fact, it's this interactive feature that sets a blog apart from a traditional website (although you can have similar features there, too). A customer who reads and responds to your blog not only becomes more loyal to your business but even more involved with the world surrounding it. They also get to know more of your other customers, thus building that "community" online and adding to that ever-elusive "word of mouth" about your shop.

Content beyond advertising

A blog or social network site gives you opportunities to help the local community, too, which most business owners consider good for business. By promoting local events in blog entries, links to related association and organization sites, and reports on competitions, elections, and promotions, you help build the fan base as well as encourage your customers who participate as competitors. A substantial side benefit is that your business enjoys some of the same "halo effect" that an event sponsor gets—at considerably less expense.

What else can you do on your blog? How about a virtual swap meet where your customers (and your shop) offer used equipment, excess supplies, or even advice or labor? You can also offer a "tip of the week" for do-it-yourselfers. A real no-brainer is to encourage customer questions that you answer for all to see. Job postings—both help wanted and situation wanted—can be popular, useful entries. Many blog servers allow you to display picture and movies, too, so you can encourage customers to send you digital files of ways they've used your products, events in which they participated, and other material for the world to see on your blog. The possibilities are endless.

Don't forget the advertising side of the blog, either. There should be a place for you to write about your company's history and the things you do. You can also link to your shop's conventional website, too. You might even be able to sell advertising on your blog to other local businesses as well as to your vendors.

How easy is it?

Getting started is so easy it's almost ridiculous. I went online, found a blog-hosting service, enrolled, and published a free blog in less than three minutes!

I went to www.blogger.com (a service owned by Google) and followed the very simple on-screen instructions. The first step was to register, giving them nothing more than a user name, password, and email address (which they pledge to keep confidential). The second was to name the blog and the third was to choose a template from the dozens offered. Note that no money changed hands—a feature I greatly appreciated. The next screen was where I posted my first entry and, bingo, I was a blogger!

Adding the bells and whistles like posting photos to your blog takes a little more time, but they're well worth the trouble. There's even a feature, called AudioBlogger, that lets you call from any phone and post a message to your site as an MP3 audio file. How cool is that?

Facebook is even easier in many ways, although building a sizable list of "friends" can take some time.

A few caveats

Naturally, there is a downside to blogging and social networking (isn't there always?). For one thing, it may be cheap and easy but it's not automatic. Someone has to set up and maintain the blog, which takes some time and effort. The more of each you put into it, of course, the better impression you'll make. The more bells and whistles you add, the stronger the blog's appeal—but also the more work you'll have to put into it. Photos have to be made web-compatible, links to other web sites should be updated, and, assuming you allow customers to add their messages to yours, you need to police the blog diligently to prevent unwanted entries that can cause embarrassing problems. Most sites allow you to "moderate comments" to control what appears under your name.

And, like anything else on the web, a blog's popularity is directly related to how well it's promoted. If you have a customer email list, start by sending them all a note announcing your new blog and inviting them to check it out with a link embedded in the message. Register the blog with some of the online blog directories, which usually offer listings in various categories (often free). Put some flyers up at local gathering places, too. Once you've got it up and running and are happy with the growing content, send a press release to all your local media—they're often interested in this newest development in the online world.

If putting your business into cyberspace has seemed like more trouble than it's worth, maybe now is the time to reconsider your decision. A Facebook page or blog is cheap, easy, and can be a very effective marketing tool.

Chapter 17

Social Media Marketing:
Facebook, Twitter, and LinkedIn

"Your business can establish a two-way dialogue with customers that reinforces your marketing message."

If your company isn't doing the Facebook Fandango or Twitter Tango, you're not dancing to the tune of modern marketing. Social media isn't just for playing online Scrabble and posting pictures of drunken college buddies. It's the latest instrument in the savvy marketer's orchestra.

"Literally all of our clients use social media," says Co-Communications President Stacey Cohen, whose Mount Kisco, NY-based twelve-person firm represents dozens of companies and organizations of all sizes in Westchester county and beyond. "It runs the gamut from occasional usage to concentrated utilization where social media is their main communication portal." In addition to web designers, writers, and videographers, the firm even has one person on staff whose primary job description includes writing and posting "tweets" for their clients' Twitter accounts all day.

For the uninitiated, Twitter is one of three major social media networks currently in use (although at the rate of change in the online world, there could be three new ones by the time you finish reading this chapter). The other two are Facebook, home of a half-billion online profiles and some of the greatest time-eating games since Microsoft included solitaire in the first version of Windows, and LinkedIn, a service where individuals can post their professional accomplishments and network with potential clients, customers, and/or employers. Other social media with business-building potential include MySpace, MerchantCircle, Ziggs, Ryze, Fast Pitch, and Biznik, whose snappy slogan is "Business networking that doesn't suck."

All these and more are online social networks that business owners like veteran restaurateur Isi Albanese use to build their customer base. His popular family restaurants—Bellizzi of Mount Kisco and Bellizzi Larchmont—are perennial "Best of Westchester" winners and have a devoted following Albanese thought had room to grow. His strategy? Social media.

"I have three sons and I know how kids communicate now—through texting, through Twitter, and through social networking sites," Albanese says. "They read restaurant reviews on blogs and have Facebook pages. So does my wife. I wanted to try it for my business."

Albanese already had a website, but under the guidance of Kristen Ruby, President of Ruby Media Group in Waccabuc, NY, he added Twitter, Facebook, and YouTube to his marketing arsenal. The results were impressive. Traffic to the Bellizzi website increased by 30 percent, from about 2,800 visitors in the third quarter of 2009 to 3,700 in third-quarter 2010. The restaurateur used social media to introduce a brand-new product: his Spa Vento line of salads made with fresh, locally grown organic produce. Within the space of a few months, the new salad line accounted for an additional $10,000 per month in sales for the Mount Kisco restaurant. That's a lotta lettuce.

Such results aren't automatic, of course. Nor are they cheap. Although the media itself doesn't cost anything, there is time required to set up the online accounts and portals, not to mention the significant amount of time to produce and distribute content. A Twitter "tweet" may be only 140 characters—about 20 words—but coming up with something fresh, catchy, and relevant several times a day 365 days a year is no cakewalk. And if you don't keep your social media up-to-date, it can reflect on your business as badly as a window display coated with dust. Firms like Cohen's and Ruby's can help, but they don't work for free.

It's also essential to respond quickly to the feedback social media generates. That is, after all, the biggest advantage of the social media strategy: your business can establish a two-way dialogue with customers that reinforces your marketing message. When someone "friends" you on Facebook, you need to welcome them—personally and quickly. That's also the biggest difference between traditional advertising and social network marketing. Advertising is all about making sure the largest number of ears and eyeballs are exposed to your one-way selling message. Social media marketing relies on one-to-one networking in a series of two-way conversations. The two approaches—advertising and social media marketing—are complementary, not exclusive.

It's a big old social media world out there, but here is an overview of the three main outlets and how many progressive, aggressive businesses are using them.

Facebook for fun and profit

Facebook is the big kahuna of social media. With a claimed 500 million users worldwide, it allows a business owner to communicate in numerous ways with seemingly everyone on the planet. It also happens to be the brainchild of a Westchester native, Mark Zuckerberg, who was born in White Plains and grew up in Dobbs Ferry. Facebook is more oriented toward personal entertainment, but more and more businesses are using it as part of their marketing effort.

Like many business owners, Lance Cerutti of Suburban Wines started with a personal Facebook page, then converted to a business page. He's very active in online social media. "We blog, have a Twitter account, and post a lot on Facebook and Flickr, where we can display photos as well. We also send out a daily email newsletter about wines we're tasting, what's on sale, and things like that. The Facebook page is an extension of that. We try to connect it all together as the persona of the store."

Cerutti's use of social (and other) media mirrors the character of his 54-year-old Yorktown Heights, NY, business. "We have always been the type of store where we work with our customers to match wines with what they're eating, what their palates are, what their interests are. We're all wine geeks in the store. We thought the social networks would allow us to do the same thing."

There is a lot to say about wines, so creating content isn't difficult, according to Cerutti. The hard-core customer is also passionate about the subject, so they welcome the information regardless of how it's delivered. "We never post about sales or hard-sell messages like that. I don't want to be in people's faces all the time. We talk about wines we're tasting or about the big renovation the store just went through. We don't post much that requires people to reply. We might put an event up, but don't expect people to sign up or anything like that."

Cerutti, like most Facebook-using businesses, doesn't expect to reach new customers through social media. Instead, he focuses on building a relationship with his current ones. "Facebook supplements what we do. It has not replaced anything. We still advertise in the print media and send out our daily email."

Getting started on Facebook is easy, as is connecting with people who become your "friends" for a personal page or "fans" for a business page. Watch what you wish for, though. When I created my personal page, the first "friend" to find me was an old flame from college who had become a religious fanatic during the intervening years. She repeatedly urged me to go on a spiritual journey with her to Israel until I figured out how to block her messages. My wife found the whole thing quite amusing.

There are other potential hazards with online marketing, according to Jamie Nicastri, General Manager of The Gym in Armonk, NY. "With all the social media, I am concerned about how you control your reputation," she says. "It's never been a problem here, but I try to watch how the gym is portrayed on the personal Facebook pages of the employees. That opens up a whole Pandora's box of legal issues. We have regulations in our employee manual on how they can depict the gym and we ask that they not put our logo up there."

Nicastri is a big fan of Facebook, however, and uses it as a big part of The Gym's communication strategy with the help of Co-Communications. "We've had websites since we opened the clubs but we started about a year ago on Facebook. We have an in-house IT person who updates our website once a month. Facebook is much easier to do." They update Facebook every week (if not more frequently) and combine it with YouTube videos to encourage frequent page visits by customers. "We might do a lower body workout," she explains. "We'll videotape that and post it on our Facebook page. It then gets picked up on YouTube and our website."

The big advantage of Facebook is that every time a "friend" or "fan" signs in, they see the content you've posted on your business's page, according to Anthony Maucieri, owner of East Hills Cabinetry in Briarcliff Manor, NY. "Facebook keeps us at top of mind for our clients." He says. "It has substantially increased our referral business. I can't give you numbers, but whenever I check the source of a referral, it's almost always from one of our 'friends' on Facebook. That's the power of it, keeping us top of mind."

Maucieri says he gets a lot of mileage out of Facebook's visual presentation. "Instead of having to update our website every time we do a job, I can post the photos on Facebook. A lot of our clients are proud of their kitchens, so they send the link to their friends."

Like most other things business owners do, success with Facebook or any other social media isn't automatic. "It's important to stay on top of it," Maucieri says. "Time is in short supply for business owners, so it's a temptation to let it slide. But if you don't keep your Facebook page updated, it can hurt your brand—you look stale." His solution? "To do a quick update doesn't take long. You just have to write three or four lines. I link to a lot of articles online, which delivers something of value to the customers. That makes you a resource for the homeowner."

Twitter your way into your customers' hearts

At first glance, Twitter doesn't look so much like a resource for anyone as like a barely comprehensible stream of drivel inflicted on the Internet by spelling-impaired typists. But it's not—really. Actually, Twitter is a promotional tool used by an increasing number of tech-oriented businesses.

To the cognoscenti, Twitter is a social networking and "microblogging" service whose users send and receive 140-character messages called "tweets" among their "followers" (contacts in Twitter talk). What can you say in 140 characters? Things like "@marketingfool has gr8 idea 4 nu #bizbook on selling by RT. 2 c vid, http://bit.ly/cINTug. May b pyramid scheme, esp part bout 1 + 1 = 3 as long as no 1 gripes. cha think?" Translation? Don't ask—just go with the flow and read the next tweet that comes across your computer screen, PDA, or mobile phone. If you really want to know more, click on the link "to see the video."

Linda Rey, who runs the Sleepy Hollow, NY, insurance agency founded by her father in 1978, swears by Twitter, although she uses Facebook and LinkedIn as well. "It's all about engagement and interaction, getting people interested and remembering who you are," she says. " My Twitter name is @ReyInsurance. I Tweet everything from photos to noise in my head. I keep it clean, civil, and fun."

Rey does it all herself, spending about 90 minutes creating and posting content every day. That's a significant chunk of any business person's schedule, but she points out that it's spread throughout the day. "When you think about it, before there was social media, you went to networking events," Rey says. "There is the money for the events, then the time you spend away from your office or your family. The payoff is the same, too." You meet people, they get to know you, then hopefully they will remember you when they need you. "Social media networking is no different from going to an event," she says. "I can't afford to be the 'best kept secret' so we still do a lot of face-to-face networking at Business Council and Westchester County Association events." She is also past-president of the Tarrytown Chamber of Commerce, is active in the local chapter of the American Association of University Women and helped found an organization for entrepreneurial women in the county.

The key to Twitter (and other social media) is the number of followers, friends, fans (or whatever) the business can attract. Internet marketing consultant Stacy Solomon of Briarcliff Manor says two good ways to attract followers on Twitter are to use plenty of relevant search terms in your profile and to use "hash tags" (the number symbol on the keyboard) before keywords in your Tweets. She explains, "That way, you and your messages show up in searches by potential followers." She also recommends scanning Twitter for conversations you can join. Your comments will hopefully create interest—and followers.

All that time in cyberspace has paid off for Rey, who says, "We do get leads and referrals from people who have seen us online. I even wrote a business insurance policy that came through a Twitter follower located in Texas. We've written a couple of auto accounts, a retirement account, homeowners insurance, even a flood policy directly as a result of our online presence."

LinkedIn leverages your connections

Business-to-business marketing has a place in the social media scene, too. It's current home is LinkedIn, where 75 million professionals, executives, freelancers, and just regular human beings are registered in hopes of establishing profitable relationships with others of like ilk. The site's more serious mission is reflected in less Twitter-like gibberish and fewer Facebook distractions like games and other folderol. It's more like networking on digital steroids.

Dominck Crea started the PSP Group in 1999 as a payroll processing company. Today, the Mamaroneck, NY-based operation has 16 employees and provides a full range of human resource services including benefits administration. He's a great believer in networking—face-to-face and online—and belongs to several groups on LinkedIn. "Groups" are basically on-line clubs where people with like interests exchange opinions, advice, gossip, and all the other tidbits of communication that make the business world go 'round.

"I take part in the discussions going on," Crea explains. "For example, one group member posted a question about overtime and how it is treated in New York and asked if other members had any trouble with audits. I just offered some advice based on my experience and the member loved that. He ended up calling me and I turned it into an account. I wasn't pitching anything. I was just trying to help him solve a problem."

In 2008, Crea started a LinkedIn group aptly named "Westchester County Business Owners." Today it has 280 members who post information about their businesses, pose questions, and keep blatant sales pitches to a minimum. Crea also says the group is great for the master technique of networking, referrals: "If I see in a forum that someone is asking about a type of service—say they need a printer—I try to put them together with someone I know in that business. It's kind of a pay-it-forward thing."

Tips From Social Media Pros

"You have to create a plan. I see many professionals and smaller businesses who haven't looked at their objectives. Who is their target audience? What key messages are they trying to get out?"

--Stacy Cohen, Co-communications

"A great way to gain followers on Twitter is to Retweet what someone else has to say or to jump into their conversation and add your own perspective. Also ask people to retweet your links by adding the words 'Pls RT'"

--Stacy Solomon, Internet Marketing Consultant

"If you are spending five hundred to a thousand dollars each month on marketing and take even one or two months of this and invest in setting up your social media, you can see a significant long-term gain for your business."

--Gerald Stern, WOW Production Services

"One hundred high-quality followers easily equals one thousand so-so followers, because in the social media world you want people to constantly pass on the things you write, as well as send you material to post. Business people must avoid an overt 'sales' method—you'll just turn people off and you'll lose your following."

--Chris Cornell, TwitterProfessor.com

"You should never expect social media to be completely cost-free. Someone must spend time staying on top of all those tweets, messages, Facebook updates and blog posts. Likewise, quick (if not instant) replies are necessary to maintain a reputation for responsiveness."

--Kristen Ruby, Ruby Media Group

Whether they pay-it-forward or pay-as-they-go, more and more business owners and managers are turning to social media networks for very good reasons. "In the current economic downturn business owners must go above and beyond to promote themselves," says Rye NY Chamber of Commerce Secretary Sally Wright. The organization received dozens of requests for a repeat of its recent social media seminar. She adds, "Social media is one great way to accomplish that."

Chapter 18

Specialty Market Case Study:

Automotive Aftermarket

"You can use tried-and-true marketing tactics
like showing off your work at neighborhood cruise-ins
but the main thing is to go after the business."

When business is good, many auto shop owners might be tempted to rest on their order backlogs and cruise to prosperity. The smart ones, though, know that if you don't market your services today, you may not have customers for them tomorrow. The question most of them are asking isn't whether they should promote, it's how.

Chris Sutton, whose family has operated the Street Rod Garage in Grant, Alabama, for 25 years, says even after their best year ever he swung into the next year with an aggressive two-pronged marketing strategy. The Street Rod Garage is a full-service operation doing scratch builds, restorations, and restyling in three buildings plus a 1200 sq. ft. retail showroom.

The first part of Sutton's strategy is to exhibit at some of the larger car shows, possibly including the nationals. He's done local and regional events in the past, but feels it's time to expand his market. "We've found the bigger bucks are out there," Sutton says, "We just have to reach out to get them." Exhibiting at shows is a tried-and-true strategy followed by automotive restylers around the globe.

Shows around the web

The second prong in his attack, though, isn't quite so common. Sutton put a website up in 2003 and says, "I've been extremely pleased with it. We've done local work for years and years but since our website launched, we've got customers from all over the world. We're seeing customers we never would have seen without a website."

The site, www.streetrodgarage.com, sells everything from performance parts to custom chassis, has a free classified ad section where customers can offer everything from used parts to used rides, and lists local and national events information. It brings in shop customers as well. "The first call that I got from our website was a complete rebuild on a 1940 Chevrolet sedan," Sutton says proudly. The job was worth tens of thousands of dollars.

Sutton does all the web work himself. He drew up the plans for the site and hired someone else to build it, but he now does all the updates and changes. "It's a lot of work. I spend almost as much time working on the website as I do working on cars," he observes. "A few years ago, I never would have thought it." He has several site upgrades on the drawing board for the coming months.

Sutton isn't the only shop operator turning to the Internet to draw customers. Bernie Myers, owner of the Hot Rod Barn in Morris, Illinois, built his website himself using off-the-shelf software a couple of years ago. He estimates that he got a dozen jobs off the web last year. "People are accustomed to going online for shopping and doing research. If you've got something there that people can see and it interests them, that helps you get people through the door, too." The site is www.thehotrodbarn.com.

Myers does hot rod fabrication, custom paint jobs, chassis, springs, and exhaust work, and just about everything else except upholstery with six employees in an 8500 sq. ft. shop. Business is strong, too, Myers says, main-ly due to the baby boomers: "A lot of people are at the age where their kids are out of the house and they've got a little spend-able cash again, so they're building the car they had in high school. They have the money now to get their toys back. Baby boomers are wonderful people."

Myers uses the Internet to not only bring in new customers but to strengthen relations with his current ones as well. "Customers can come and look at their cars on the website instead of having to visit the shop. They can check progress on the job and see the kind of work that we do. The Internet's been a good tool."

The website is about the only kind of advertising Myers does. "When we moved to our new location two years ago, we did some newspaper and radio ads, and handed out a lot of flyers at car shows and cruise ins. Initially we hit it pretty heavy but today, 95% of our work is from referrals and regular customers."

The personal touch

Mike Mauldin, Sales Manager of the Sachse Rod Shop in Sachse, Texas, says they're planning an increased presence at car shows including national events staged by the NHRA. They're also planning to attend more local and regional events. "Usually we take a car that we're working on or a chassis that we're building just to let people know that there is somebody local that does that kind of work," he says.

The Sachse Rod Shop does custom paint, body and chassis fabrication, glass, and interiors. Their retail parts sales operation has grown to about 50% of total sales in the last eight years, largely through a growing catalog effort. The 167-page catalog is available online at www.sachserodshop.com, but Mauldin says they encourage customers to contact them via telephone to make sure the parts are what the customer needs.

"What a lot of customers tell us they really like is doing business with somebody that knows what they're talking about," Mauldin says. "We have experience with the parts that we're selling. We can answer a lot of questions that people can't get answered anywhere else."

Another reason Mauldin wants customers to call before ordering is to confirm prices. Demand for steel is causing a ripple effect on pricing through the aftermarket business. "I get a price increase almost weekly from different manufacturers because steel is going up so much," he says.

Now is the time for aggressive shop owners to cash in on the growing market of baby boomers (and others) eager to drive down the street in a ride totally different from every other vehicle on the road. You can use tried-and-true marketing tactics like showing off your work to car owners at neighborhood cruise-ins or take it to them around the globe on the World Wide Web (or both!) but the main thing is to go after the business. Who knows, you might find the customer like the one Mike Mauldin describes:

"We're currently working on a high-end '55 Chevy. The customer expressed to us that he wants it to win street machine of the year. He doesn't care what year. Every now and then you'll run across a customer with unlimited resources."

Chapter 19
Specialty Market Case Study:
Sports Team Sponsorships

"The marketing essence of sponsorships
is the endorsement value that the investment gives you."

When it comes to sponsoring sports teams, it's all about R.O.I. Return on Investment. Put another way, what's in it for me?

That's the crux of the matter for most automotive performance shop owners when local race teams or car owners come calling to ask for money—or other kinds of help—to fund their endeavors on the track or strip. But it's hard to say no, especially when the guy making the proposal is also a customer or even worse, a friend. "We probably help too many guys," says Buzz Nye, owner of Lucky's Speed Shop in Mulvane, Kansas. "It's hard not to."

Lucky's is a 5,000-sq. ft. shop with a 1,000-sq. ft. showroom that specializes in performance work. Without general garage work to fall back on, the shop needs all the support it can get from local hot rodders and works hard to earn their support. "The business is very, very competitive," Nye says. "The mail order people make it almost impossible for us. So we have to be competitive in that arena, in the pricing, but what we have to help our customers to learn is we can add something to the price of what they pay for a part."

Sponsoring race teams drives home that point, according to Nye: "I help a young man here, Frank Carson, who races at nearby 81 Speedway.

We provide tune-up advice and motor help." When Carson wins, Nye says, "He'll say it runs so good because Buzz down at Lucky's put the tune on it." This demonstrates their in-shop marketing message: "Our experience may help them realize they need a different component from what they think they might need. It's due to having done this a long time and having a lot of experience here in our shop; being involved with racers."

The marketing essence of sponsorships—whether you put your money into race teams or the PTA bake sale—is the endorsement value that the investment gives you. There is, hopefully, a halo effect in which the potential customer's good feelings about the sponsored entity transfer to your shop or product as well. And if the customer admires and wants to emulate them, all the better. That's why golf club manufacturers shower golf pros with free clubs, balls, and shoes. But is the halo effect enough?

Value outside the track

"It's essential to show the sponsor that you gave them value for their money," according to Tony Thacker, VP of Marketing for So-Cal Speed Shop, which is headquartered in Pomona, California. "It's very difficult to quantify the return on sponsoring somebody else's race team effort," he says, "unless you know that they've got the wherewithal to give you the return that you need." So-Cal's high-profile involvement with racing dates to 1946. Thacker points out putting a decal on the car is just the tip of the iceberg when it comes to giving value to the sponsor. "In our own race effort, we send regular reports out to all of our sponsors and we try real hard to get stories on the race car in different magazines. Typically, other people don't do that. Professional racers do, but the typical people calling us don't realize that that's the more important part of the job."

That's probably why so many shops don't feel they get full value for their sponsorship dollar. At the track, their sponsorship identification competes for the fans' attention the same way the race teams vie for the lead—and there's a lot of smoke, dust, and noise getting in the way of both. A productive sponsorship will also generate publicity outside the track environment, with personal appearances, endorsements, and other news-worthy events. That's what drives the maximum return on investment.

Stephan Bastrvycki, owner of Fast Line Motorsport in Canton, Connecticut, understands the quandary: "It's a hard thing to put a number on. It's sometimes hard for the company to have those costs justified." He goes on to observe, "It's just like advertising is in any case. It's hard to say, for example, when a company puts an ad in a magazine, how many people it's really reaching."

Use target marketing

That doesn't stop Bastrvycki from investing in racing, although he spends his money on his own team. He runs a Honda Prelude in World Challenge Events, which closely matches the demographics of his market. "It's a great place to promote what we do," he says. "A lot of our customers are in the import market. We have a lot of Hondas that come in the shop for dyno tuning. The series itself is basically geared toward the sport compact car, so it's an ideal place for us to advertise."

So-Cal builds race cars for individuals and OEM's and the only race car the company currently sponsors is a roadster owned by Thacker and another associate, Jimmy Shine. Does the company plan to sponsor any race teams? "It would depend on what the offer was," Thacker says. "We get approached all the time by people thinking that we've got tons of money and that we could sponsor their race car." It's not likely, though.

Beyond the decal

You should get more out of sponsoring a sports team than a decal on the car or a logo on their shirts. Here are some of the things you can ask for:

- Pictures of the team in action that you can use in your advertising.

- A letter from the team thanking you for your support that you can post in your business, use in other advertising, and attach to proposals when you give them to potential customers.

- Personal appearances by the team members—and their equipment—at your shop. You can promote the appearances with direct mail, email, or even newspaper ads as events where fans can "meet the pros" while they inspect your business.

- Distribution of frequent press releases—identifying your shop as a team sponsor—on event results and team developments.

All of these things will help the team, too. Remember, sports teams depends on fans just like a business depends on customers. The more fans the team attracts, the greater the value of the sponsorships it sells.

Intangible ROI

Buzz Nye says he'll keep on sponsoring race teams because of the very positive word-of-mouth it generates for Lucky's. "They tell the other guys that we're good guys and we're good people to work with," he says. It doesn't have to be costly, at least the way he approaches it. In addition to the dirt-tracker, he sponsors Chris Brown, an NHRA racer in super comp dragster who was number seven in Division Five last year. Lucky's has sponsored the team for four years, providing parts instead of cash. "We don't have a lot of money in this business to hand out," he says.

Nye is like many performance shop owners when it comes to return on investment: sometimes the intangibles are the most important. He says, "It's instrumental that the local shops be involved with the racers" because racing is "a red-blooded American thing. That's what we love about it." When it comes right down to it, Nye sponsors race teams for the best reason of all—because he wants to. He says, "We like to help our racing buddies."

Chapter 20

Business To Business Marketing –
Beyond the Price Sheet

"You should market to other companies
much the same way you market to consumers:
with a combination of advertising and personal selling."

When it comes to bringing new retail customers through the door, most small businesses rely on a combination of word-of-mouth, a little media advertising, and appearances at trade shows and other events. Ask them what they do to build their business-to-business sales as subcontractors or suppliers for other companies, and they tell you it's all about price; marketing doesn't matter.

But they're wrong. While price is certainly a major factor in attracting wholesale or subcontract business, it's not the only way. In fact, even if you offer the lowest prices in town, you need to do some marketing to your prospects to let them know that! While you're at it, make sure your business-to-business marketing message contains the good word about the quality of your work or merchandise, your willingness to stand behind it, and how happy it makes the end-using customer.

You should market to other companies much the same way you market to consumers: with a combination of advertising and personal selling. In many ways, it's easier, too, because you generally don't have to explain your product or service in quite so much detail and there are a smaller number of prospects, so you can more easily tailor your message to each one. The main thing to remember, just as in retail marketing, is that your message needs to be repeated consistently and constantly over time. Marketing is not a one-shot deal.

Non-junk mail

Advertising to other companies doesn't mean running TV spots in the Super Bowl. It's much more targeted than that, which means it's much more economical. Direct mail is probably the single most effective medium to use; it's intrusive and there's very little waste circulation. There are three keys to successful direct mail: a good prospect list, a compelling message, and repetition. You can make up a short prospect list yourself if you spend a little time with the Yellow Pages. Just look up the dealers and other prospects in your market area, call them to get the names of the general managers, service writers, sales managers and buyers, and you'll have a solid prospect list to work with. Keep it handy, by the way, because you'll use it later when you start making sales calls.

The direct mail piece itself doesn't have to be a four-color glossy catalogue. In fact, a one-page *personal* letter introducing you and describing how you can make money for the other company (in one form or another, that should always be your pitch) will be a good place to start. Every three or four weeks, send another one saying the same thing in different ways. You can announce new equipment or product lines you've added, quote a recently satisfied customer, or brag about any awards you've received. Address it to each individual on your list, keep it to one page, include a picture or two, and make sure you send something at least once a month.

A web site is a useful business-to-business marketing tool, too. If it has plenty of pictures of your work, testimonials from satisfied customers, and some information about your background and your company's capabilities, it will give the prospect even more reasons to send business your way. Also make sure there is a *working* email link, phone and fax numbers, and keep it all up to date. You don't need to hire a high-priced web designer, by the way; most hosting services offer perfectly good bare-bones templates. The site itself can cost less than $10 a month.

Face-to-face

Once you've done a few mailings, go visit the prospects on your list. Before you go, though, think through what you want to say to them. A short (three-minute) description of what you do and how you can help the prospect's company make money will get you started. Once you've delivered it, ask them what you need to do to get their business, then shut up and listen. Nine times out of ten, they'll tell you what you need to know as long as you use a professional approach and demonstrate a willingness to pay attention. Don't be offended if you get a brush-off or two and don't give up if they say they already have a preferred source for what you're trying to sell. If that happens, thank them for their time and move on. Keep them on your mailing list, though, and visit them again next month—things change!

You should also have a leave-behind of some sort for every sales call. This can be a version of your latest direct mail piece, a fancier brochure, or even a coffee mug with your logo. And don't forget to give them your business card. In fact, one of the best tactics you can adopt is to always hand out two cards at a time and ask the recipient to pass one along to anyone else they know who might be interested in your services.

Once you've established a relationship, build on it. There are all kinds of creative things you can do to keep your company at the top of the prospect's list of preferred subs and vendors. Offer to sponsor a sales contest for the prospect for example, awarding a prize to the dealer's salesperson who sells the most pieces in your line during a given period of time. Watch for the prospect's own sales event, then have a pile of pizzas or a few boxes of donuts delivered with your compliments on their busiest day. If the prospect belongs to a civic group or supports a local charity, become involved with it yourself. The goal is to keep your name in front of the prospect all the time.

Your own vendors may help you with business-to-business marketing, too. Many manufacturers and distributors have co-operative advertising programs that pay part of the cost of your printing and mailing if you feature their products. Even if they don't have a formal program, it doesn't hurt to ask the next time you place an order. Others may have regional sales reps who would be available to go with you to make face-to-face calls. You should also ask if your suppliers do any lead generating of their own—trade shows, magazine advertising, etc.—that they can share with you.

Even with help from your vendors, marketing isn't free, of course. A hundred first-class letters will cost you at least $100 for postage, envelopes, and computer printer ink. Imprinted coffee mugs aren't cheap and even a supply of business cards will set you back a few bucks.

The biggest expense, though, is your time. Someone has to compile the prospect list, write the sales letters, and make the sales calls. In most small businesses, that someone is you. To control that particular expense (and to make sure the marketing gets done), dedicate a set number of hours every week to it, budgeting your time the same way you do your money.

Marketing is an investment from which you should expect a return. Fortunately, results from business-to-business marketing are usually easy to track. There is a finite prospect list, you know exactly how you're marketing to each one, and you can easily identify the orders that you get from them. Make the investment in business-to-business marketing for a few months, then review the response. You might be surprised how much your company's business has grown.

Chapter 21
Speaking Up For Your Business

"It's good for business because the more information and knowledge you give your customers, the more they appreciate it."

"Friends, collectors, art lovers, lend me your ears" is the mantra of gallery owners who use speaking appearances as opportunities to market their galleries, promote their artists, and further the cause of fine crafts in their communities. It's a tactic that's surprisingly under-used, considering its effectiveness and cost-efficiency. It's also one that's very easy to adapt to other kinds of businesses.

"If I go out to an arts council or to another non-profit, it puts me in a different setting and I get to reach a different audience," says Catherine Bert, owner of Bert Gallery in Providence, RI. In addition to appearances like these, Bert also does academically-oriented lectures on Rhode Island artists, often in conjunction with local institutions like the Rhode Island School of Design, and makes presentations at her gallery that coincide with the six to eight exhibits she holds every year.

Bert also helped found Gallery Night Providence several years ago. It's a collaboration of twenty-five different venues from museums to small, artist-owned galleries built around adult-education programs where people have the opportunity to directly experience the visual arts. "We might do a lecture on woodcuts or I might have an artist come in and do something on certain facets of jewelry making," she explains. "That is a very public, free event that we do for a very broad community."

Why does she do it? "It takes a lot of time, but I consider it part of my promotion of the gallery. I consider it a much more cost-effective way to reach audiences. They get to understand what your knowledge base is so that, if they're interested in acquiring in an area, they know you have an expertise." She adds, "It also gives them an opportunity to see the gallery in a non-commercial setting."

Efficient marketing

Theresa Abel, who purchased The Artisan Gallery in Belleville, Wisconsin, after serving as its art director for several years, is just discovering the marketing possibilities of public presentations. "We started," she says, "with a show by Sally Holl, a woman working in pastel and monotype. She also did some etching and worked with a lot of printmaking processes. The general public doesn't understand processes like that nearly as much as oil painting or watercolor." A Madison, Wisconsin, art group heard about the exhibit and called the gallery to see if someone could give them a brief program about the artist. "We gave them a short presentation on printmaking," Abel says.

Because she was already familiar with printmaking and the artist's work and was used to speaking to people about her, it didn't take long to prepare the forty-five-minute talk. "People don't usually spend that much time in front of a given artist's work," she points out. About thirty people came to the gallery for the program, which also made it a very time-efficient way for Abel to communicate with a lot of potential customers at once.

Many galleries will present short talks during openings or have artists on hand to demonstrate a given craft to passersby, but Abel believes the formal presentation setting lends an important aspect: "At openings, you can get a lot of people, but if there's someone talking, they may sort of listen for five minutes as they walk by and they may not be that interested."

They lack the depth of involvement that attending a lecture or workshop requires.

How do you get started? Bert suggests working up a presentation well in advance as part of your exhibit planning process. This allows you time to gather interesting material and promote the event right along with the exhibit itself. In terms of reaching outside the gallery, she says, "Many non-profits have speaking programs that they're interested in getting new speakers and new ideas for. It's very easy to hook up and find people." Another place to look are colleges, especially those that offer adult-education programs. If you don't feel comfortable going it alone, you might also get together with a few other galleries and develop a lecture series.

Stage fright is your friend

Do you suffer from stage fright? Good! You'll be a more effective speaker if you do.

I've done thousands of sales presentations, speeches, seminars, and live radio and television appearances—and I get that little flutter in my stomach, sweat on the palms, and shortness of breath every time. I welcome them as signs that my energy level is going to be high—I want the extra energy that comes from an attack of stage fright.

Stage fright is your friend—all you have to do is control it. The first step is to recognize the symptoms as nothing more than a small rush of adrenaline. The next step is to make a conscious choice to focus your excess energy on the presentation you're going to make.

To control the intensity of your stage fright symptoms before your presentation, take the physical edge off them by doing some simple isometric exercises. Press your palms together—hard—for thirty seconds. Grip the arms of your chair as hard as you can for another half minute. This will burn off some of that excess adrenaline in your system while leaving you the energy you need to convey enthusiasm.

Now take a couple of deep, long breaths, using your diaphragm to fill your lungs completely. Let each breath out slowly to a count of ten. This will steady your voice and make you ready for a powerful opening statement.

Your stage fright has now become a reservoir of energy that you can tap into when you need it. You'll find that you're better focused and your presentation will be much more dynamic. You've made stage fright your friend.

Public speaking isn't everyone's forte, but most gallery owners are like Abel, who says, "I love talking to people about the work if they're really interested." She suggests turning that skill into group presentations because, "It's good for business because the more information and knowledge you give your customers, the more they appreciate it and the more they want to own a piece and take it home."

Bert takes it a step further: "People are very intimidated by the art world. They feel they are unprepared to experience the visual arts and this is breaking down those barriers. We introduce people in very non-threatening ways to the visual arts." The result is good for everybody concerned. "They fall in love with what I have been in love with for many years: creative minds and looking at ideas and objects in the world from different artists' perspectives."

Chapter 22

Tune Your Company's Publicity Machine

"Dealing with paparazzi and signing autographs
is a small price to pay for frequent press coverage
that will help build your company's business."

I bet you never thought of yourself as a newsmaker. You know, one of those people with their name always in the headlines, face on the cover of every magazine, and voice filling the airwaves with pithy sound bites. You are a newsmaker, though, or at least you can be if you spend a little time tuning up your publicity machine.

But, you might ask, who needs all that fame and glory, anyway? If you are a business manager or owner, you do. Every time your company gets mentioned in the press, potential new customers hear about you—many of them for the first time. Previous customers get a reminder, too, and both may find a reason to visit your business and open their wallets. In its simplest form, publicity serves as (almost) free advertising.

Press coverage of your company helps build your business in other ways, too. Employees like it, since everything that burnishes your shop's reputation makes them shine a little more brightly, too. Vendors are more likely to sharpen their pencils for a customer with a high profile and even bankers look more favorably on someone who has the respect of the press.

When current customers read or hear about your company in the media, it validates their decision to do business with you and increases their loyalty to your shop. It also makes them more likely to pass the word along to their friends, so you could say that press coverage supercharges good word-of-mouth.

Every business owner or manager I've ever interviewed recognizes good word-of-mouth as essential to his company's success. It works because, unlike paid advertising, the source of the message is supposedly objective and their endorsement of your work is trustworthy. A story about your business in the local newspaper has the same aura of believability. The difference is, instead of one person telling one other person, press coverage is one person telling a whole bunch of other people at the same time.

Create press coverage

So, how do you go about getting all this wonderful media coverage? Through a consistent, professional public relations campaign. You can retain a PR firm to do it for you (an expensive option), do it yourself if you've got a way with words, or hire a freelance writer (and/or photographer) to produce the material and handle distribution of it to the media yourself. The size of your budget and the amount of time you can devote to the effort are obviously big factors in your decision.

The heart of the publicity process is the press release, a simple document (really!) that tells the media the story you want them to cover. You should send out a constant stream of press releases about everything that happens in and around your business. If you sponsor or participate in associations, clubs, or trade shows, you have an endless supply of topics. The same is true if you support any charities or worthwhile causes like disaster relief funds, local or national.

But there are also newsworthy events happening right in your business every day. Did you hire a new technician? Issue a release announcing your shop's expansion. Customer's garden win a flower show? Spread the news to his or her hometown media as well as your own. Add a new product line or shop machine? Tout the upgrade in one of your press releases and get the company you bought it from to issue their own as well. Celebrating your tenth anniversary in business? Long-term employee retiring? Successfully complete a technical workshop? All of these things and more are reasons to issue a press release.

There are plenty of books with instructions and sample press releases at your local library, but if you consider writing a grammatically correct sentence similar to massaging your own forehead with a ball peen hammer, consider finding a freelancer to do the writing for you. For a surprisingly nominal fee, they'll gather the information the release should contain, write the page or so of text, and put it in a format the media outlets can use. To find one, try posting a notice at your library, calling the English department at your community college, or checking with your chamber of commerce. You don't need to make any long-term commitments, so try two or three different writers until you find somebody you can work with.

A thousand words

Provide photos along with your press releases as often as you can; they will increase your press coverage. Assuming you use a consumer-grade digital camera, here are some guidelines for publication use:

- Use highest resolution setting on your camera
- Use highest quality JPEG setting
- Use auto white balance and ISO
- Save files with the least amount of compression
- Don't retouch or process the files
- Burn the photos to a CD and send it along with your press release—or email them.

You can hire a freelance photographer if you're not comfortable behind a camera. Quite frankly, though, most news media aren't looking for

114

great art—they just want a clear photograph that will reproduce well, preferably with people in it!

Media relations

You can generally handle the distribution of the releases yourself. Once the writer gives you the copy, put it on your letterhead and send it to every media outlet you can think of. Again, your local library can help you find their addresses and contact information. The obvious ones include your local newspaper and radio stations, but don't forget the broadcast and cable television outlets, too. You never know when they're going to be in the market for a visual story featuring a snazzy product. There are also weekly papers and free tabloids as well as regional magazines, organization newsletters, and even websites and blogs devoted to local news in many communities. All of these outlets consume huge amounts of content, so they're always looking for new sources of material.

Try not to limit your campaign to one type of news. Certain editors will be receptive to technical stories about new products and services, but business editors like to hear about expansion and hiring. Consumer affairs editors look for news that will help readers save money, while lifestyle editors want features about interesting people and their flashy lives. Every mention of your company's name is a plus.

Another reason for you to distribute the releases (and to list yourself as the follow-up contact on the release), is that most reporters will call you to get more information to shape the piece to their specific readership. The electronic media will certainly call, because they'll want a sound bite or video clip from you to go with the reporter's story. Even if the media doesn't pick up a particular story from your release, it may spark a related idea they want to pursue and they're likely to turn to you as a source if they have your contact information on file.

When the media call, talk to them! They're usually working against a deadline and can't spend a lot of time waiting for you to return their calls. For the same reason, they also won't take up a lot of your time.

Being a newsmaker does have its drawbacks. But dealing with paparazzi and signing autographs is a small price to pay for frequent press coverage that will help build your company's business.

Section Two

Advertising:
How To Grow Your Business
With Ads That Work

Chapter 23

The Advertising Conundrum

"If you stop promoting, your customer base melts away
like an ice cream cone on a July afternoon."

Plenty of small business owners consider advertising a total waste of money. According to them, word of mouth is the best advertising and that's something you can't buy. They're right, but only partly: word of mouth is the best, but you *can* buy it. That's what good advertising does—it buys word of mouth.

A good, targeted ad starts potential customers talking about you. It gives them something to think about and prompts them to bring you up in conversation with their friends and neighbors. If you don't advertise at all, you're really just hoping for two things. First, that you satisfy all of your customers all of the time so none of them have anything bad to say about you (remember, word of mouth cuts two ways) and second, that a whole bunch of them will spread the word on their own. That's a lot to hope for, which is why most banks don't accept deposits of hope.

Keep in mind, that "advertising" doesn't have to be a million-dollar TV commercial on American Idol. A fifty-cent postcard announcing your new selection of life-enhancing widgets mailed to a targeted list of a couple hundred potential customers is advertising, too. It's the kind of advertising that buys some word of mouth.

"We all buy ads with the hope that it's going to get us customers," says Bill Colton, "but there's certainly no guarantee on that." Like many other small business managers, Colton has personally experienced that sad fact of business life for more than 25 years as the owner of Troyer Speed & Custom in Rochester, New York. But that doesn't mean he's going to stop promoting his business. He says if you stop promoting, your customer base melts away like an ice cream cone on a July afternoon.

When to advertise, how much to spend on advertising, even whether to advertise at all are questions that are at best difficult to answer for businesses in the automotive performance industry (or any other). On the one hand, you like to think that your reputation for good work and fair prices will draw people into your shop. On the other, you have to realize that if they don't hear about you in some way, that elusive new customer isn't going to even know you exist, much less that you have a strong reputation. And when you factor in all the competition you face, advertising becomes much more imperative.

"Everybody in the industry is working on thinner margins than they did ten years ago because it's such a more competitive business," Colton says. In order to maintain a satisfactory level of profit on smaller margins, your sales volume has to increase. Existing customers have to be persuaded to spend more money and new customers need to be attracted to your shop. And look out for customer attrition, Colton advises: "The mail-order deal, the Internet thing, and all the above just keeps nipping away at your customer base so you have to become a little bit more aggressive."

Linda Hietala, who owns Reliable Welding & Speed in Enfield, Connecticut, with her husband Brad, agrees that you have to keep trying to attract new customers. "The best form of advertising is word of mouth and referrals," she says, "but you can't totally rely on that. You need to be in different publications so people can find your name and phone number."

Different strategies for different shops

So how do these advocates of small business advertising go about it? Hietala believes in the scattergun approach, using as many different promotion vehicles as she can afford and not relying on any single medium to hit all the targets. "We try to reach everybody in every different way," she says. Reliable advertises in Speedway Scene and regional racing papers and also does track programs and similar publications. She's also a believer in the Internet.

"We have the website, of course, and people can request catalogs and so forth. That helps us in other than our local area." But, she adds, the web works in mysterious ways: "A lot of times, it helps, too with some of the local people. They can go on there and check to see if we're carrying a certain product line or different things like that." Hietala's experience with the Internet jives with the results of a study done by Valentine Radford Advertising in Kansas City, which showed that about two-thirds of the time a shopper will research a product online and then buy it in the store.

Reliable has been on the web for many years, and so has Troyer, which Colton says was one of the first speed shops in the area to go on-line. He believes there's a great future in it, but points out one of the Internet's biggest problems: the time, effort, and money required to do a good job with it. "We've been undergoing a long process building a website," he says. "We were one of the first in our area to have one, but we just never put the dedication and the expense into making it a good site. We try to work on that, but it's a matter of time and money."

Ah, there's the rub: Time and Money. Colton observes that all advertising requires generous applications of both. He'd particularly like to do more direct mail advertising, which he says has been successful for him in the past, but, "When you start coming up with ads and things like that, you almost need a full-time employee dedicated to making flyers and coming up with programs. That becomes costly in itself. The cost of mailing is expensive, then the cost of the thought process of what to do and how to do it and then making it, it just becomes very costly."

How about other advertising media? Neither Hietala nor Colton have had much luck with broadcast media like radio, television, or cable, probably because, as Colton says, "You'd be reaching maybe ten people out of five thousand that might be prospective customers. It's just such a cost to reach those ten people."

Results, please

Hietala adds, "Some things you stop doing after you evaluate what you get from them versus what it costs to do it." She's believes in constantly assessing how well her advertising performs: "Whenever we can, we try to ask new people how they heard about us. A lot of times, when they call, they'll just mention where they saw us." That's not a foolproof method, of course, since many (if not most) customers don't really know how they heard about a particular business because they're bombarded by so many advertising messages every day. If they don't know, they're also inclined to say the first thing that pops into their head rather than admit they don't know, a phenomenon which can badly skew your results. That's why Hietala gives each promotional outlet plenty of time to prove itself.

Like many speed shops, Reliable and Troyer are heavy supporters of the local race scene. "We have a forty-foot parts trailer that we bring to one of the local race tracks," Hietala explains. "That's a good way for us because the track (Stafford Speedway) has, in addition to their weekly racing, special events through the year where they're bringing in other touring series like the featherweight modifieds and the Busch North. This last year, they had an open wheel show with the midgets, sprint cars, and super-modifieds. So being visible there with a trailer, we're reaching a lot of people." They also sponsor the rookie program at the track and provide contingency awards for special events like a 100-lap race. Troyer sponsors a night at Lancaster Speedway, a big asphalt track in the area and gets involved with small promotions with other tracks as well as running his own car.

While these advertising opportunities are specific to speed shops and other automotive-related businesses, many similar ones exist for small business owners serving other markets. Many pet shops support their local animal shelter, for example, and clothing retailers are often big sponsors of local fashion shows. With a little imagination, business-to-business firms can use the technique, too, like when accounting or law firms offer free seminars to local chambers of commerce or provide speakers for service clubs.

Colton says he firmly believes that one of the keys to success in advertising is consistency: "When you see repetitive ads, people start getting used to it and it registers. When they think they need a particular aluminum rod end, they'll think of one brand that they've seen repeatedly in a magazine. That's when you start to see payoff."

Chapter 24

Advertising Goals, Part One – Your Image

"The goal isn't to enhance the image—
it's ultimately to affect the bottom line."

Let's talk about your advertising. Why it works and why it doesn't work a lot of the time. We're going to start by talking about the three basic advertising functions, the goals that advertising can accomplish for the advertiser. These are image goals, sales goals, and positioning goals. These are not mutually exclusive and certainly many ad messages accomplish or attempt to accomplish more than one. But, for clarity of presentation, we're going to discuss them one at a time.

Image advertising goals are those sort of warm, fuzzy, amorphous ambitions that many advertisers have. They want people to feel good about their business or good about their company.

We hear many times that one medium or another—television or magazines, for example—are the great image building media. For many years, the Television Bureau or Advertising, the trade association responsible for promoting commercial use of television, went around telling advertisers to use TV to build their business' image while using the newspaper to generate specific price/item sales.

And there is no question that television is the great image medium. Beautiful sunsets, puppies and little girls frolicking through a meadow of wildflowers can't be presented very effectively in a black and white newspaper ad. But keep in mind that those kind of images don't sell a heck of a lot of merchandise, so image advertising needs to be used with great care.

There are some businesses that have a legitimate need for image advertising. They have a real need to put out the message that "Hey, we're great people here at Company X!"

They key to doing this kind of advertising is to start by answering the question, who are we trying to influence? Who is the intended recipient of our message?

Defining the audience

Legitimate image advertisers almost always have a very specific and narrow intended audience. They're trying to reach those individuals who have a legitimate concern with the type of company they're doing business with. These will tend to be companies like financial institutions, public utilities, health care companies, certain manufacturers or others who have very specific image problems.

What these companies are trying to do is influence the attitudes of the people in the well-defined community they are trying to reach (with community meaning simply a discrete group of individuals, not a geographic area). The people they are trying to reach will have some influence on the success or failure—the economic health—of the advertiser's business.

Let's look at an example: a manufacturing company with a plant located on the river in your town. The company manufactures widgets and as part of their manufacturing process they paint those widgets. An unfortunate by-product of the painting step is that they use a lot of solvents, which, in the days before the EPA, were dumped in the river.

The current owners of the company and their management and employees didn't do this—it was a previous generation. But the bad will created by this action exists today. And that bad will interferes with the company's ability to hire people, to sell the widgets, and to raise money for operations. Maybe the bad will gives the town a bad name, which in turn drives away potential contributors to the tax base, which results in the widget company's taxes being higher than necessary. In short, a bad image problem can affect the company's bottom line.

And that's at the root of addressing an image need through advertising. The goal isn't to enhance the image—it's ultimately to affect the bottom line. The bottom line can mean either profit and loss or it can mean the value of the company as a possible acquisition candidate or on the stock market. The image itself has no value of its own. You must make sure that connection exists—that the image advertising has a direct connection to the company's economic value.

And you can't make that connection unless you know whose mind you're trying to reach with your image advertising. Very seldom should the intended target be the community at large. It's almost always a much narrower focus. Let's look at some of the narrower communities where image needs might exist.

The company's employees are a frequent target. If the employees feel better about their company, they're less inclined to do nasty things like go on strike, more apt to work harder, and less likely to leave for greener pastures, among other things. That's why you'll often see companies advertising a year or so before their union contract negotiations begin. They want to soften up the opposition. That's why you see those seemingly purposeless ads that say, "Welcome to the ABC Widget Company. We're a wonderful place to work. We're so proud of our many great employees who contribute so much to our company and the town in the which we all live." Didn't you every wonder why a company would spend money on a campaign like that? Wonder what they were trying to sell?

The company doesn't care what you, the casual viewer, thinks about them or their ads. What they care about are the 5,000 people who work in their plant who will sitting across from management at the negotiating table in a year. They can't very effectively address them directly with the message about company love, but they can obliquely get the message across through such image ads on TV.

Good citizenship

Sometimes advertisers spend to influence even smaller groups, like government regulators. If you're in one of many kinds of regulated businesses, like public utilities, insurance , or telecommunications, your ability to make a profit is highly dependent on the attitudes toward you held by the public service commission or insurance commission or other regulatory body that governs your business. That group of five, ten, or fifteen citizens holds your fate in the palm of their hands. Among other things, you may have to go to them every year or so and convince them that your company is a good citizen and deserves to make a larger profit than you did the year before.

The commission studies your books and compares your operation with others and considers all sorts of factors before they make a decision about the level of your profitability. One of the key factors they consider are the number of complaints received about your company's operations from the community! So if your company's advertising can influence the number of complaints filed by your customers, you come out ahead.

One of my favorite examples of this type of campaign is the spring staple presented by the local light and power company. Every March, you'll see a few ads warning kids to keep their kites away from the high tension lines. These aren't to keep kids from being electrocuted—the power company has liability insurance to protect itself—but rather to convince the community that it cares about all those rosy-cheeked citizens of tomorrow. It makes a great story to present to the public service commission when they can show the amount of stockholder money spent on public service ads instead of dividends.

The personal touch

There's another audience that image advertisers sometimes try to influence, but it's one that they don't talk about much. In fact, they're usually not even conscious of their attempt to reach them. Many times, image ads are directed at the advertiser's friends and acquaintances! If you're the only bank in town that doesn't advertise on TV, you may feel somewhat self-conscious at the country club when your peers and competitors are talking about their TV campaigns. There's some keep-up-with-the-Jones' in business life, too.

These are the same advertisers who star in their own commercials. Or put their dogs or their grandchildren on the screen. There are a few, like the iconic Dave Thomas of Wendy's, where the persona meant something to the consumer and the product sold better because of it. But the vast majority of those self-aggrandizing ads don't inflate anything except the advertiser's ego.

The danger of all image advertising is that it doesn't directly influence the sales or other revenues of that company. That's why, when times get tough and profits erode, the first thing that gets cut is the image advertising. Which makes you wonder why it was done in the first place, doesn't it?

Another problem with image advertising is that the results—even in terms of attitudinal change—are very difficult to measure. And an advertiser should know what you're getting for your dollar. It's hard enough to track response when you're doing something tangible like running an 800 number that takes product orders in direct response to an ad because there are other factors that influence the purchasing decision. But with image advertising it's almost impossible to measure the results.

Chapter 25

Advertising Goals Part Two – Your Sales

"Advertising is about sales, sales, and more sales."

It's been said many times and it's very true. A retailer has three goals:

1. To get a potential customer into the store
2. To get them to spend more money while they're in the store
3. To get them to come back to the store again

In one way or another, all advertisers—retail or otherwise—want to accomplish the same things. Ultimately, advertising is about making sales, sales, and more sales.

Every retailer wants to do one thing—BLY—Beat Last Year. That's why nearly every store manager can tell you to the penny what they sold on a given day last year and how this year's same date stacked up. Technologies like networked electronic check-outs give this data to the minute.

Why is that? Why is selling more necessary? If you made a nice profit by selling $10 million last year, why do you have to sell $11 million this year? Is it because you're greedy? That's part of it. So is the inflation factor and its effect on operating expenses even when it's low. But the real reason is that growth is what drives our economy. If we're not growing, we are indeed going backwards. There is no such thing as stasis in business. If you're not beating last year, you're losing ground to the competition. You're shrinking relatively, and that will eventually lead to serious problems in your ability to survive. You'll lose the whole $10 million in sales if you don't at least try to get $11 million.

There are other reasons for a constant growth strategy. Many publicly traded companies' stock prices are propped up by analysts' and investors' expectations of continuous growth. If the forecast earnings don't show growth, the stock price collapses. And why does a company exist? To enrich it's stockholders. If it doesn't do that, through either price appreciation or dividends, its management gets punished (both directly and indirectly) by a falling stock price. If you ain't growing, you're dying. And stockholders punish managers of dying companies. You may not be a publicly traded company, but you probably compete against several of them. And they are driven to take your sales away if you don't use every tool at your disposal to compete with them—including good advertising.

Growth improves margins

Then there's the third reason that increasing sales are important. Sales growth generally improves the profit margin of most businesses. Net profits will grow at a faster rate than even sales if there is stability in the fixed costs (the overhead) of the business. Sales growth, as long as it's not generated by excessive price cutting, increases both the absolute amount of the company's profits and the percentage those profits represent of total revenues (the gross margin).

Every retail business has basically two categories of expenses. There are fixed costs, such as the monthly rent on the store space and the utilities. And then there are the costs of goods sold, or the price paid by the retailer for the merchandise to be sold. While there certainly are volume discounts given by manufacturers to retailers, the unit cost of goods sold doesn't change much as sales go up and down. But with the fixed expenses, the larger the sales volume, the smaller the percentage of sales they represent, and the greater the profit margin. This can be expressed in another way:

you are amortizing your overhead across a wider sales volume, thus creating a larger profit margin.

Increased sales volume generally also means a faster rate of turnover of the inventory, which in turn reduces carrying costs. Almost all inventory in most stores is financed in some way, either by the retailer's vendors or the bank, so if the goods can be sold before they rack up large interest expense, the profit margins will be wider.

Media and sales

Let's detour for a minute to talk about ratings and circulation—the numbers that media sellers generally quote to persuade the advertiser that they deserve the lion's share of his or her ad dollars. Just like with any other kind of data, there are right ways and wrong ways to use them. The wrong way is how most media salespeople do it, which is to choose media (or sell it) based on who reaches the largest audience. Everybody has to be number one—have the largest circulation or reach—and lots of advertisers think they have to be on the number one medium.

You'll hear things like, "Our station is the number one station in town. We reach 90% of the homes in our town every week!" Sounds impressive, doesn't it? Translated into hard numbers, it's just as impressive. If there are 160,000 homes in the market for example, then this station reaches 144,000 of them weekly. If the newspaper circulation in that town is 48,000, then you'd reach three times as many prospects by advertising on the station with the big reach. The logical conclusion, of course, is that you'd also sell three times as much merchandise. And if the costs are the same, the advertiser would be foolish to spend money in the newspaper when the TV station reaches so many more people.

But those expectations of tripled sales are unrealistic. Advertising doesn't work that way. Most advertising doesn't create demand. It doesn't move a customer to buy something he or she wasn't in the market to buy in the first place. What it does do is direct the buying behavior of the customer that is in the market to buy a given type of product or service to buy from a particular vendor or to buy a certain brand. It's more a matter of timing than of reach. Putting the advertising message in front of the consumer who is actively in the market is more important that putting it in front of more people in total.

Of all the people in the market, only a finite number are considering the purchase of a given item at a particular point in time. The advertising media chosen, or the selection of the number one station instead of the number two station, won't increase that number. All it will do is set up some unrealistic expectations in the advertiser's mind that sales are going to be higher depending on the reach of the medium chosen.

That's why consistency of advertising is important. Different consumers enter the market over time, so it's important to have your message there when they are. On-again-off-again campaigns miss potential consumers and so does placing your ad one month in this medium and next month in another one.

All media in a market reach basically the same consumers. The same people who read the newspaper in town also watch the local TV stations and listen to the local radio stations and drive by the billboards. The audiences of each medium are not mutually exclusive! And generally, the difference between the number one station and the number four or five station won't be nearly as great as you might think. Since those differences are almost always fully accounted for in price differentials, your best advertising buy will usually be the one that focuses your message on the consumers most likely to buy and keeps it in front of them over the longest period of time.

That's what ratings and other audience data are for, to give you guidance in scheduling the most effective ad placement to reach your prime customer most efficiently. I would rather reach a slightly smaller number of customers more often by concentrating my advertising on the second or third-rated station than reach more customers fewer times by using just number one.

The message means more than the medium

Even more important is to consider the advertising idea rather than the media numbers. When we think about ideas, we're going to create some more tangible, reachable goals for our advertising. Start not by considering which station reaches the most people but by identifying and profiling the customer most likely to buy your product or service. Be as specific as possible about the prime prospect. Go beyond age and sex demographics. Thank about that customer's lifestyle. The number of kids they have, what kind of home they own or apartment they rent. Where are they in the stages of life? Building a nest? Emptying the nest? Retiring? Create a mental image of that best potential prospect—the person who accounts for the largest portion of your sales—and then figure out how best to reach that one person over and over again.

If your advertising idea is designed to appeal to that best prospect, you'll produce sales. And, since all the media reach that one prospect anyway, choose the one which reaches him or her most often. Repetition and being in front of the customer when they're ready to buy are what makes a good advertising schedule. Knowing what motivates the best customer to buy is what makes a good advertising idea.

Chapter 26

Advertising Goals Part Three – Positioning Your Business

"Once the consumer puts an advertiser in a position,

it generally stays there."

The third type of advertising goal is really the most important. That's positioning the product or service in the consumer's mind. Positioning is particularly important in the context of having your message in the consumer's mind when they enter the market with the intent to buy.

Positioning strategy deals with the factors that influence customer choices. Why does the customer buy Coke instead of Pepsi? Are there reasons for that choice? Aren't they both essentially the same product? In blind taste tests can people really tell the difference? Most can't, but there are still decided preferences for one brand over another just as there are decided preferences for one store over another. And positioning theory addresses those preferences by looking at the factors that influence the decision.

Positions are the qualities that the consumer thinks about, or attaches, to each competitor in a category. They're things like quality, service, price, selection, friendliness, convenience, etc. The consumer places each competitor in the category in rank order in each of the pertinent qualities, thus giving each advertiser a position in their mind. The relative importance of each position—is price more important than quality when buying a loaf of bread, for example—dictates the consumer's choice of product.

And that can change with time, even with the same consumer. Where I live there are two grocery stores within convenient range. One has a slightly better selection in certain product categories and the other has slightly lower prices. Which store gets my business on a particular day depends entirely on which position—selection or price—is more important to me that day. If we're entertaining important guests that night and want to feed them a fancy meal, selection rules. If my kids are coming to visit and I need to fill the fridge with junk food, guess what? It's going to be price.

A point to note is that whether one store actually has better selection and the other lower prices isn't relevant. What's important is what I perceive to be true. Once the consumer puts an advertiser in a position in their mind, it generally stays there.

The most important position

Some positions are more important than others, of course. The one that matters most is the position that the best consumer holds as most important. In other words, the prime consumer we talked about before, who represents the largest single share of sales in the category, may well consider one quality—service, let's say—more important than any other. Even if other market segments think price is tops, or selection, or convenience, the advertiser should be almost exclusively concerned with just the first position. He'll get more business from the best consumer—and therefore more business overall—if he can occupy the position as the best service provider in that consumer's mind.

Let's do some share of market math to prove this theory. Assume the best consumer generates 60% of the sales of product A. The second-best accounts for 30%, and the third 10%. In nearly every category, by the way, that's the way it works out. The so-called 80-20 rule isn't a figment of the cliché writer's imagination. If you aim your ad message at the best consumer and get 50% of her business, you'll secure 30% of the total market (half of 60%). If you aim at two other targets (hard to do at the same time, isn't it?) and get 50% of their business, you'll only end up with 20% of the total. The odds are with you when you advertise strictly to the best prospect.

Many business owners believe that price is the most important position to every consumer, so they assume that by trying to gain and hold the position as the price leader in their category, they'll garner the largest share of market. That's why almost all advertising says we're the lowest, we're the cheapest, we won't be undersold. But that's the wrong position to try to hold most of the time. Consumers in almost every category very seldom make price the number on reason that choose one store or brand over another. That includes some categories that you would think are automatically price sensitive, like supermarkets or department stores. The number one reason consumers choose supermarket A over supermarket B is cleanliness! Followed by selection. Price comes in third or fourth!

Most people choose a particular bank not because they get a lower loan rate or a higher interest rate on their savings account, but because it is the most conveniently located in relation to where they get paid.

Defense versus offense

It all comes back to knowing which position is most important to the prime consumer. Remember, positions are easier to defend than they are to conquer. Most advertisers should determine the position they hold and then capitalize it rather than try to be something they aren't in the consumer's mind. Advertising works but it doesn't work miracles. If you have the selection position, don't give that up to try to knock off the price leader. You probably won't win their customers but you could easily lose yours in the process.

Television is the great positioning medium. It's greatest strength isn't its massive reach, it's the medium's ability to position a product in the consumer's mind. Almost all of the great advertising campaigns you can recall were TV campaigns. Think about some of the positioning statements you've heard on TV. "The Uncola." "I'd like to teach the world to sing." "Winston tastes good…." You get the idea.

Advertising ideas create the images, feelings, attitudes, beliefs…the positions in the consumer's mind. So where do we get those ideas? First we establish a goal: What position to we want to create, what action do we want the consumer to take? Then we beg, borrow, steal, or create an idea to accomplish that specific goal.

Chapter 27

Where To Find Advertising Ideas

"The best approach is to be as specific as possible
in the claims presented."

If you're at a loss for something to say in your ads, one way to begin is by "borrowing" someone else's idea. Let's take a few common advertising themes and break them down into a couple of the categories I've been talking about (images and sales) so we can see how the advertiser's goals are accomplished.

Begin with image-enhancing ideas. Remember, the most important consideration here is the audience we're trying to reach or the community we're trying to affect. Have you ever seen an ad where a company spends money to tell people how they are spending other money to help out a charity or a worthy cause? How about Procter & Gambles' support of the Special Olympics? Or the PGA Tour's many ads pointing out that a significant portion of the revenues earned by their golf tournaments goes to support various charities? Why do they run those campaigns?

Both organizations are genuinely trying to help. They truly do believe that successful businesses have an obligation to give something other than products, profits, and jobs back to the communities they serve. But they also believe that their potential customers will view their products and services more favorably if they believe that a portion of the profits generated by their purchases go to support worthy causes. If you have to choose between two equally-priced and otherwise similar tooth pastes, wouldn't you just as soon buy the one that also sends some potion of the purchase price to a worthy cause? It's part of creating an overall favorable image of the company and its products or services.

How do you use the same tactic as a local business? Can it be enhanced? Let's take the case of a local community bank—if there are any left. And let's not forget to specify a goal; in this case, to improve the bank image among corporate customers. Notice how we've identified a particular market segment (corporate bank customers) rather than the public at large.

One way the bank can improve its image is to choose a local cause—like the town art museum—and mount a campaign to raise funds for it. The bank offers to not just make a donation itself, but to match donations made by others (up to a set limit) during a specified period of time. What's in it for the bank? The biggest benefit is the good will created in the minds of their best customers. The corporate leaders in the community are probably also the supporters of the local art museum. In most towns, the public at large doesn't spend a lot of time or money on museums, but business leaders do for various reasons. And they're the ones the bank is trying to reach with the message that the bank cares about the same causes they do.

And why advertise it? Why not just make the donation and bask in the glow of a good deed well done? Because the glow is a heck of a lot brighter when more people see it. And the best way to make sure the largest number of people see that glow is to advertise it.

This type of promotion also creates a feeling of camaraderie among the other donors and the bank. It builds a general belief that they're all in this together which will hopefully carry over into their feelings about the bank and their future banking needs. It's an image of the bank as one of us who demonstrates the best side of all of us to the public. The campaign makes the intended target—the bank's corporate customer—feel better about themselves.

As a side note, many times a local media outlet will participate in the charity benefit promotion by donating some ad time or space or giving some sort of discount in return for identification as a co-sponsor. This can be either a positive advantage or a negative disadvantage if it dilutes the value of the promotion to the advertiser. The media are generally swamped with requests for such deals, however, so don't expect to get immediate acceptance if you take them such an offer.

Another type of image promotion is the achievement recognition campaign, in which the advertiser tries to create an affinity between their business and the public accomplishments of someone in the community. "Student Athlete of the Week" and "Teacher of the Year" fall into this category. The advertiser gives a small award of some sort to the person honored and buys the publicity for the award on the media.

Employee recognition is closely related. In an age of decreasing employee-employer loyalty and a shrinking skilled-labor pool, retaining and motivating good employees is becoming increasingly difficult. If the company's best employees are publicly praised for their accomplishments in the company's advertising, they will, hopefully, feel more positively toward their employer. Such campaigns also help companies attract new hires as well.

Sometimes the employee recognition campaign can reinforce a consumer benefit as well. A restaurant chain that promotes friendly service can prove that claim by recognizing the wait-person who knows the greatest number of customers by name. Or the realtor who puts a picture of their top producer in the newspaper is not only recognizing that sales person but promoting the rapid turnover of their listings at the same time.

Public safety campaigns are yet another form of image advertising. The beer industry's drink responsibly campaign is a prime example of a public safety campaign. It's directed to two audiences. The first is the beer consumer, who will hopefully observe its urgings to drink less today so they can live longer to drink more tomorrow. The second audience, though, is the real intended target of the campaign, and that is composed of the members of the regulatory bodies who might have an interest in restricting beer advertising or beer sales in a way that would damage the industry's business.

All of these ideas-and the hundreds of others that you will think of—satisfy a need that is only indirectly related to the immediate economic health of the sponsoring business. While they may have some impact on the general public, they are usually aimed at one particular audience that may in fact be a very small one. Image advertising has its place, but it's essential that the specific goals of the campaign be clearly identified in order to cost-justify the effort.

Sales-promoting ideas

How about some ideas to build sales? The supply of ideas here is nearly limitless, but the inventory of ideas is tapped so frequently that there are very few truly original ones. We're going to briefly cover some of the principle types and give a few examples of each.

Theme sales are everywhere. Anniversary sale, Presidents' Day sale, Back to School sale, the Boss is Gone sale. Every major holiday and a few imaginary ones are excuses for having a sale. So are important dates in the company's history, like the boss's birthday, the anniversary of the big fire of '06, and the ever-popular grand-reopening sale.

Price and item advertising is another sales-generating approach that's used and abused widely. Consumers are very jaded by such offers, especially when they're couched in "percent off" terms. They've also come to expect that the sale price of a given item is probably the real everyday price, so something stronger has to be presented in order to overcome their skepticism. The best approach is to be as specific as possible in the claims presented such as, "Our widget are now on sale for $9.99 and they are available at that price only until Friday." The consumer assumes that since those specific facts can be checked easily, they must be true.

Contests are good traffic generators. Come into our store and register to win a vacation. Put your business card in the bowl and win a free lunch. Radio stations are famous for running contest after contest for themselves and their advertisers. Often the media will provide the prizes—or structure the deal so that they're buying the prizes from their sponsors. Contests are fun and can be good traffic builders if they are fresh, different, and run for a short time. The entry period has to be close enough to the awarding of prizes to prompt consumer action now. The prizes have to be enticing enough to alter the consumer's behavior. And the contest has to be simple enough to not block someone from entering.

Many businesses give away items like coffee cups or tote bags. Such premiums aren't bad, but they can be expensive on a per-customer-reached basis. Good premium items have high visibility and long user life, extending the exposure of the advertiser's message over as long a period of time as possible. Unfortunately, in this day when logos are on everything from our clothing to the fruit we buy in the grocery store, premiums have lost a great deal of their effectiveness. Many advertisers also make the mistake of offering premiums without advertising them. In other words, they reward their current customers with the free stuff (which isn't bad in itself) but they forget to let non-customers know that there's yet another reason (the free stuff) to come to their store. Once again, identifying a clearly defined goal for the campaign is an essential part of the planning process.

Loyalty programs or frequent buyer rewards are increasingly popular, driven in large part by the ever-decreasing cost of data base marketing systems. You can get airline miles for buying just about anything these days. But there are other variations on that theme that serve the same purpose, which is to get the best customer to buy ever-increasing quantities from the sponsor. Shopper bonus cards, punch cards giving a free item after the purchase of a set number of other items, percent of purchase rebates after multiple purchases are all forms of the loyalty program.

Cross promotions, which carry customers from one business to another, can be very successful. The video store that gives take-out pizza coupons. The restaurant that sells discount theater tickets. The carpet store that gives a coupon good for carpet cleaning. These are all examples of ways two different businesses can cross-promote, share the cost of the advertising, and produce an ad campaign that's greater than the sum of its parts.

You should never be at a loss for something to say in your ads. Just look around at the thousands of advertisements you see every day and borrow one you can adapt to your business goals.

Chapter 28

Five Rules For Effective Advertising

"You must know what matters to your customer
before you can produce advertising that appeals to them."

Effective, results-producing small business advertising isn't impossible, it's just hard. It's hard to make good ads, it's hard to buy efficient media, it's hard to judge results. But it's not impossible. All you need to do is follow these five simple rules.

Rule One - Know your customer

Who do you sell to most of the time? Let's say you operate a garden center. Are your best customers apartment dwellers or home owners? Are their homes on small lots or big acreages? Are they do-it-yourselfers or do-it-with-helpers? Obviously, each of these customers needs different things from your nursery. They also need different advertising strategies for everything from copy points to media selection. You simply can't be all things to all customers and neither can your advertising, so the first step in good marketing is to define the customer who puts the most money in your till every month.

You'll want to know their age, sex, and income, for starters. Even more important, of course, is their housing situation, lifestyle, and family mode. You can commission expensive market research to find out these things, but you probably know much of it already from your daily dealings with them. The key is to focus your advertising on those best customers—and only them—instead of trying to be all things to all people.

Rule Two - Get their attention

We're assaulted by literally thousands of advertising messages every day. On TV, radio, and the newspapers, to be sure. But also on every package in the supermarket, bumper stickers on almost every vehicle, and logos on a remarkable amount of clothing. They all blend together and become background noise in the life of today's over-stimulated consumer. If your ads blend into the background, they don't do you any good.

You'll go a long way toward grabbing the consumer's attention if they know you're talking only to them, hence the emphasis on Rule One. It also helps if you have an attention-getting device, whether it be a ringing telephone that begins your radio spots or a screaming headline at the top of your newspaper ads. You have to do something to make your tree stand out from the forest.

Rule Three - Sell a benefit

The only thing most retail ads tell the customer is what the store has to sell. And the only reason they give the customer to buy it is because it's on sale that week. If the customer doesn't want, say, a bag of weed killer, the ad is meaningless to them. Or, if they do happen to be in the market for some lawn chemicals that week, the ad gives them no reason to buy it from that particular store other than price.

To break out of that trap, make sure your ads emphasize the benefits of buying from you. Don't tell the customer what you have; tell them what you're going to do for them. Talk about how buying a tree from you will lower their home's heating or cooling bill, increase their home's value, and give their kids a shady place to play in the summer. Offer to add value to their purchase by teaching them how to plant that tree or how to care for it. When you tell the consumer what's in it for them when they shop at your garden center, you greatly increase the likelihood that they'll respond to your ads.

This goes back to Rule One, of course. You must know what matters to your customer before you can produce advertising that appeals to them. If your best customers are empty-nesters without kids, for example, that picture of little girls having a tea party under the tree you're trying to sell won't work.

Rule Four - Leave a reminder

The best advertising works in the future. Since the customer doesn't necessarily need a garden hose the day he or she sees you ad, you want them to remember you when they do. That's the function of a memory trigger in your advertising—so the customer will think of your store first when they have a need to be satisfied. A memory trigger is a element that links the benefits the customer wants to receive to the ones you offer. It can be a logo, a jingle, or even a slogan that sticks in the customer's mind long after they see or hear your ad and pops back up when they need what you have to sell.

The perfect memory trigger means something to your best customer. Let's say that your best customers are suburbanites with kids. A logo featuring a little girl holding a flower might well resonate with them. If the memory trigger also echoes the benefit featured in your ad copy—in this case, perhaps it would be the family values inherent in gardening—it will work even better.

Rule Five - Buy media right

There are two basic elements in the practice of advertising, the message and the media. Newspapers, direct mail, radio, television, the Internet, and the yellow pages are just a few of the media you can choose to put your message in front of the customer. You can spend buckets of money on advertising space and time and you can invest countless hours analyzing the arcane data that supposedly tells you how to do it. Or, you can simplify the process—and improve your results—by going back yet again to Rule One.

If the medium you're considering doesn't reach your best customer, there's no point in buying it. If the medium you're considering reaches your best customer but a whole bunch of other people as well, make sure you don't pay for all those extra ones. When comparing media cost efficiencies, the only number that counts is the number of best customers you reach for each dollar you spend.

Finally, when it comes to scheduling your media exposure, keep in mind that customers tend to respond to the most recent ad they've seen. Memory triggers notwithstanding, the freshest impression is the strongest one, so you want it to be yours. Since it's tough to predict exactly when the customer is going to be in the market for something, it's advisable to run your ads as constantly as possible. Budget so you can heavy-up during peak seasons, of course, but don't make the mistake of advertising only at those times.

Like any set of rules, any one of these five can be parsed, bent, or even broken, but it's hard to say what will happen if you do. Also, like any rules, they're not necessarily easy to follow. If you observe them, though, it's a safe bet that your ads will draw more customers with more money in their pockets into your store. And doesn't that make it worth the effort?

Chapter 29

Effective Advertising Is Local

"Like politics, all good advertising is local."

Did you hear a loud flushing sound today? That was the sound made by most of your advertising dollars going down the toilet.

If you are like most small business operators, you spend a lot of money advertising your store, your services, or your merchandise. Sometimes that advertising gets results. Sometimes it doesn't. You can't really tell, but you very strongly suspect that most of your advertising doesn't bring customers through the door.

You know what? You're right! Most local advertising dollars are wasted. Why? Because very little local advertising uses effective techniques.

There can be several simple reasons for this problem, but one of the most prevalent is the use of national techniques in local advertising. If you've ever tried to improve your advertising results, you probably read books and articles or took courses about branding, positioning, and consumer psychology. If you dug a little deeper, you found out about market segmentation, market share and share of voice, and media reach and frequency.

Understanding all these concepts is essential—if you're a laundry detergent manufacturer. Unfortunately for most local retailers and other small business owners, nearly all advertising education and information is about how to market nationally distributed goods and services. There's very little information about how to motivate a customer to get in their SUV, drive to the store, and make your cash register ring—today.

National vs. local

Put simply, national advertising emphasizes the brand. The goal is to remind the consumer to choose one brand instead of another at some time in the future. It's not generally time-specific.

National advertising also usually avoids giving the consumer one piece of information critical to the buying action—where to find the merchandise. The manufacturer can't very well do that since its goods are distributed to retailers, discount stores, and big box chains—all of whom compete with each other. The manufacturer basically doesn't care where or even when the sale occurs.

Local advertising, on the other hand, should center on a call to action NOW. It's specific: come *here*, buy *this*, and reap these benefits *today*. The goal of your local advertising should be to get the customer into your store as soon and as often as possible.

Once there, you'll be able to up-sell a full range of products and services. You can add delivery and installation to their purchase, not to mention an extended warranty. You can fill the buyer's cart with related merchandise. There are countless opportunities to use your store displays, signage, and personnel to pump your sales.

Build customer relationships

One of the biggest areas of difference between national and local advertising, though, is the chance you have to establish a one-to-one relationship with the customer. The national advertiser may be able to create some brand preference, but the person who buys their product remains faceless. What's more, the national advertiser doesn't really know why the purchase was made. The manufacturer can speculate, do market surveys, and conduct focus group research, but ultimately they're still dealing with an undifferentiated mass market.

The astute retailer, on the other hand, can learn that Mrs. Jones is replacing her pachysandra bed with a shade garden this year because she's adding a breakfast nook to her house and wants to see some color from the window. You can advise her as well as sell her. You can establish an ongoing relationship with her based on trust and friendship. When you do, you'll have created loyalty that goes far deeper than any brand preference.

What does this store-based relationship have to do with your advertising? Plenty. First, of course, the relationship starts with your advertising. If Mrs. Jones learns from your ad that your store is the kind of place she wants to shop, that your personnel are knowledgeable and helpful, that the quality of your stock matches her exacting standards, she's going to choose your store over your competitors'.

Secondly, every subsequent ad she sees or hears reminds Mrs. Jones of that positive shopping experience she had the last time she visited your store. Since your best customer is a repeat shopper who visits the store numerous times for various types of merchandise, your ads keep her coming back.

Finally, a good local advertising approach can help instill the trust necessary for a long-term customer relationship. Featuring your employees— the ones your customers deal with—in your ads builds their credibility with the customers. Showing your facilities, showrooms, and even delivery trucks makes the customer comfortable with your operation. Offering classes, workshops, or other instruction establishes your store as the expert in the field.

These and other similar techniques are inherently local in nature. And like politics, all good advertising is local.

151

Chapter 30

Say It Over And Over

Again And Again And Again

"Advertising works the way the grass grows.
You can never see it,
but every week you have to mow the lawn."

A single grass seed planted by itself will not grow into a beautiful lawn. Nor will a single ad run one time send your sales soaring through the roof. But many small business operators expect it to, which makes them continually disappointed in their advertising results.

It may be because advertising is so difficult to measure or because it is such an imprecise science, but many business people have expectations of response to their ads that are way out of line with the reality of the way advertising works. Sometimes they lose faith in advertising's effectiveness and don't devote the time and effort it takes to make it work for them. The cure for both these mental states is to remember what Andy Tarshis, of A.C. Nielsen said: "We find that advertising works the way the grass grows. You can never see it, but every week you have to mow the lawn."

Regardless of the media used, advertising needs consistent exposure to the target audience over time if it is to persuade them to get out of the recliner and drive to the store. Repetition counts. The question, of course, is how much is enough? The answer, truthfully, is that nobody knows how many times an ad needs to be seen before it persuades the consumer to take action. All we do know for sure is that it's more than once or twice.

Break through the clutter

To begin with, a fair amount of repetition is necessary to break through the clamor of other ads competing for the consumer's attention. Americans are exposed to an astonishing number of advertising messages every day. Every hour you watch television, you'll see about fifty commercials and promos (many are shorter than thirty seconds), and every hour you listen to the radio, you'll hear as many as eighteen minutes of commercials. The print media aren't immune, either, since newspapers typically consist of at least sixty five percent advertising. And how many pieces of junk mail did you get today? One way to get noticed is to keep repeating your message.

Another way repetition works is to validate the claims made by your ad in the consumer's mind. When we're told it's "good to the last drop" we may or may not believe the statement, but eventually the claim registers in our mind. Then, the more times we hear it without hearing any evidence to the contrary, the more likely we are to eventually accept it as true. We become familiar with the statement and adopt it as a fact. This isn't necessarily rational, but whoever said consumers are rational?

The customer doesn't care

Another thing to remember about consumers is that, for the most part, they don't care. Choosing one brand of light bulb over another or shopping at this store instead of that one aren't major decisions to them. The level of involvement in making these choices is very, very low. Buying a car or a house is a high-involvement decision. Picking up a loaf of bread or a gallon of milk isn't. Most products and services fall somewhere in between. This low involvement factor works both for and against your ads. On the plus side, the customer is not going to spend any time questioning or disproving the claims you make in your ads, so eventually they'll be accepted as true. On the negative, they're also not going to pay a heck of a lot of attention to them in the first place. Repetition is part of the cure for this apathy.

In addition to the repetition factor that makes consistent advertising work, there is the timing factor, or when the consumer see the ad in relation to their need to purchase an item. Media consultant Erwin Ephron calls this factor recency. As he explains it, recency visualizes a window of advertising opportunity before each purchase. Advertising's job is to influence the purchase. Media's job is to place the message in that window.

The last ad works best

A common misconception about most advertising is that it creates a need to buy in the customer's mind. If you run a home improvement center in the real world, the need to buy arises because the customer's garden hose burst this morning or a skunk dug up their lawn last night. Those events are what brought the customer into the market for a new hose or some insecticide. If they were exposed to your advertising just after those things happened, they are going to be very receptive to your message. Customers tend to respond to the last ad they saw or heard in the window of time after the need arose and just before they make their decision to purchase.

Since skunks don't attack every lawn in your market the same week, not all customers know they need grub killer at exactly the same time. Some need it this week, some next week; some the week after. The week you're not advertising, you miss the chance to influence the customers who have chosen to buy that week. Sure, there's some residual effect from the advertising you did in the previous weeks, but the ad with the greatest impact is the one the customer heard most recently.

So, what does this mean for your advertising budget? Should you spend more? Can you spend less? The answer is a resounding "maybe." The amount of spending isn't the issue here. What's most important is that you find a way to advertise as continuously as possible. Generally speaking, it's preferable to spread a small budget over more weeks than to bunch it up for more exposure during a shorter period (commonly called flighting). Don't spend your entire month's budget on one full-page ad. Run one quarter-page ad every week for four weeks instead. Don't run 300 radio spots in one week, then remain silent for the next five—schedule 50 spots each week for six weeks. Or even 25 per week for twelve weeks!

This is not to say that you need to advertise at a uniform level year 'round. You should still vary the amount of exposure you buy according to the sales you expect to generate each period. Nor does this mean that you shouldn't heavy-up for a weekend sale or other short-term promotion. What it does mean, though, is that one ad by itself doesn't work. You need consistent repetition to make your advertising work the same way you need lots and lots of seeds to start a lawn.

Chapter 31

Case Study:

P.C. Richard & Sons

"Even in tough times, P.C. Richard generally
doesn't cut back much on advertising expenses."

The road to success in home appliance and electronics retailing is littered with casualties. Stalwart companies like Newmark & Lewis, Nobody Beats The Wiz and, most recently, Circuit City have all fallen victim to cutthroat competition, razor-thin margins and merciless financial markets. But family-owned P.C. Richard & Sons, a New York metro powerhouse in the business, hasn't merely survived the journey; the company has prospered over its 100-year history along that same road.

Fourth-generation company president Gregg Richard, 45, says credit is due to the simple business philosophy set by his grandfather A.J. Richard. "We care about creating a relationship with a customer based on a shopping experience that makes them want to come back," Gregg Richard says. "It's not about what we sell them today."

That customer experience comes from management attention to detail in a wide range of areas—store layout, cleanliness, lighting, displays, selection, and brands offered. It includes friendly and knowledgeable salespeople who can explain the myriad varieties of appliances and electronics. That attention to service continues after a sale, with deliveries and installation handled by the company's people and trucks. P.C. Richard employees also repair TVs and appliances in the customer's home, and computers, cameras and other electronics in two service centers in Farmingdale, New York., and Carteret, New Jersey.

As solid as the family mantra may be, there is a bit more to it than that, of course, because every business philosophy requires execution. The devil is in the details, as the old adage goes, and there are a lot of details in a company with more than $1.5 billion in sales and 2,840 employees. High-level customer service is wonderful, but there are associated expenses. Growth from a single hardware store in Brooklyn to 57 mega-stores in three states doesn't happen without expertise in real estate, finance, marketing, sales and distribution.

Success in the industry also requires prudent financial control, according to Joe Milevsky, CEO of JRM Sales & Management Consultants, Atlanta-based specialists in independent retailing. "It's a tough business," Milevsky says. "Margins are tight, and the inventories they're required to carry can eat profits very quickly. Unless they are really in control of the financial side of their business and budget carefully, they can find themselves without cash. We see an awful lot of that in the appliance industry."

Devoted to the business

Survival amid such challenges requires management to be totally devoted to the business, which pretty accurately describes the Richard family. The founder of the company was Peter Christiaan Richard, who emigrated from Amsterdam, Holland, and kept body and soul together by doing a variety of jobs, including grave digging and delivering milk, in the late 19th century. He also helped his milk customers with household repairs, a service that eventually spawned a hardware store he opened in 1909 in the Bensonhurst section of Brooklyn, New York

That same year, his son Alfred Joseph (A.J.) Richard was born. A.J. told a New York Times reporter that he started waiting on customers in the store when he was seven. In 1924 the business relocated to Ozone Park, Queens, New York, where it was squeezed into narrow storefronts housing a butcher, a baker and a shoemaker while the family lived upstairs. A.J. dropped out of school to join his father full-time in the business when it moved. In time, he insisted on adding newfangled items like electric irons to the store's inventory of watering cans and paintbrushes. He also introduced payment plans, allowing customers to pay 50 cents a week toward the $4.95 price of an iron.

Throughout its history, P.C. Richard and Sons has not necessarily been on the leading edge of retailing innovation, but it has been quick to adopt new products, policies and practices. In 1929, A.J. learned how to repair radios and opened the company's service department. "We were there to sell the first of everything," Gregg says. "A.J. sold refrigerators door-to-door when people were still getting ice delivered for their ice boxes." In the 1950s, he put a television set in the store's window so passersby could watch the Friday-night boxing matches—a marketing tactic that resulted in the sale of dozens of ten-inch black-and-white sets for nearly $400.

The company expanded throughout Queens and Long Island in the 1950s as A.J.'s sons, Gary and Peter, joined the business. Both of them did everything at one time or another, Gregg explains, from deliveries and sales to cleaning the stores. Eventually, Peter worked on the real estate side of the company while Gary, Gregg's father, was more involved in sales and operations. Peter is retired today, while Gary serves as CEO. By the 1980s the company was operating 19 showrooms in New York. In 1993, the first store in New Jersey opened. 2009 marked P.C. Richard's first foray into Connecticut.

Even as the company expanded, it remained family-owned and -operated. Peter has five children, one of whom, Peter III, is in the business in warehousing and trucking. Gary has three children including Gregg. Gregg has two sisters, one of whom, Bonni, runs human resources.

"We all grew up the same way," Gregg says. "Our fathers' lives were literally the business. On Saturdays they were always working, so we went to work with them. When I was five years old, our warehouse and store was in Plainview, New York, and the company offices were upstairs. We'd run around and look at the high loaders and hand-trucks, bother all the secretaries, copy our hands on the copy machine. Those are my earliest memories of going to work with my dad." Gary Richard, at 70 today, is very involved and knows every employee, according to his son.

A.J., Gregg Richard's grandfather, came into the office every day with a pad of paper full of notes and suggestions until his death in 2004 at age 95. That same year, Gregg was named the company's president. He had started his career by loading delivery trucks in high school, driving them in college, then worked in sales and store management. He also managed a major warehouse move from Hauppauge to Farmingdale, New York., which increased warehouse space from 150,000 to more than one million square feet. Gregg added digital cameras and cellular phones to the product lines and expanded the appliance service business as well.

Seizing opportunity

While much of the company's increase in store locations has been carefully planned to take advantage of proximity to warehouses and population growth in neighborhoods on the fringe of areas served by existing stores, there has also been a willingness to move opportunistically. "A lot of our competitors have come and gone, and we've capitalized on that," Gregg Richard says. "When The Wiz, Newmark & Lewis, Crazy Eddie [an electronics chain that declared bankruptcy after co-founder Eddie Antar was indicted on federal charges for fraudulent business practices], and others went out of business, we had the opportunity to sit stagnant or to grow and acquire new stores. We're really in the same position today."

In 2003, the company paid $1.8 million for the remnants of bankrupt Nobody Beats The Wiz, a purchase that included customer lists as well as The Wiz's names, logo and intellectual property. P.C. Richard turned The Wiz into an online vendor of electronics, computers and small household appliances.

"When Circuit City went out of business," Gregg explains, "we had some real estate opportunities that would put us in areas where we had a vacancy. We also hired some good people who became available. We were ready, and we added seven stores." Those stores were closed, renovated and reopened under the P.C. Richard & Sons name. "At the same time, we re-designed the interiors of all our stores—rugs and paint and fixtures and displays," Gregg says. P.C. Richard also got into the video game business in a very big way, Gregg says, and created a relationship with Verizon Wireless that put them into all the stores.

Peter Kaplan, audit partner on the P.C. Richard & Sons account for PricewaterhouseCoopers, explains how the company is able to expand while others are tightening their belts: They ensure that when the opportunities come up, they have the wherewithal to take advantage of them. "There's no drive to have more stores for the sake of bigger numbers," Kaplan says. "They manage with the goal to ensure that the company will still be in business 100 years from now."

Prudent use of debt, conservation of cash and reinvesting profits in the business are three key elements to the P.C. Richard & Sons' long-term strategy made possible by family ownership, according to Gregg Richard. "Each generation has lived, and treated the company, very conservatively," Gregg says. "We've always reinvested in the business and kept money in it. The rewards are that in tough times we were able to weather the storm and stand up strong. We're in a great financial position to do these things without borrowing money and loading up on debt."

Gregg adds that the company is able to adhere to this philosophy because it's privately owned. "We didn't have pressure to leverage ourselves to increase short-term returns, he says. A lot of our competitors had to do that, and when times got tough, they went away."

"As each generation came into the business, they continue to manage with the patriarchs' philosophy," says PricewaterhouseCoopers' Kaplan. "They don't let egos get in the way."

The importance of advertising

The competitive landscape is changing in the electronics industry. While yesterday's competitors may have been mostly regional chains, today's are national behemoths like Sears, Lowe's and Home Depot, not to mention nationwide electronics dealer Best Buy and warehouse stores operated by Walmart and Costco. Online shopping is a huge factor, too, especially in electronics. While everybody in the business advertises a low-price guarantee, P.C. Richard & Sons emphasizes its local roots, family ownership and superior customer service.

That need to compete with the national operators is why, even in tough times, P.C. Richard generally doesn't cut back much on advertising expenses. The company's distinctive five-note whistle jingle has been heard on New York TV and radio stations since 1987 and is now also heard in numerous sports venues, including Yankee Stadium every time a Yankee pitcher strikes out an opposing batter. Current broadcast ads are image-oriented, while print ads are heavy with price-and-item specifics. Both play up the stores' family ownership and local connection.

Salespeople are paid a draw against commissions and are known for being aggressive closers. "Most retailers in this field suffer 50% employee turnover every year," notes PricewaterhouseCoopers' Kaplan. "P.C. Richard's is much less than that. When they held their 100th anniversary gala, they spent more time recognizing long-term employees than anything else. A good hour and a half of the formal presentation was devoted to individuals who have been with them for more than 20 years."

Gregg's sister, 40-year-old Bonni Richard-Rondinello, believes employee loyalty has been a key factor in the company's success. She serves as Director of Human Resources and says that family ownership, in turn, is a key to building employee loyalty. "Employees see us walking around—the owners are flesh and blood—and know that we're as concerned about their success as they are. That gives us a competitive edge, too." Lower employee turnover, especially in sales, means lower hiring and training expenses. She adds that the stability of family ownership makes recruitment easier, too.

Will the family's continual reinvestment in the business pay off in today's economy? Gregg Richard is confident. "When customers feel better and start spending money again, we'll be ready," he asserts. "We're seeing some of that already."

His confidence is based in large part on history. "We have lived through two world wars, the Great Depression and many recessions," Gregg says. "We've always held to our foundation of taking care of the customer. There have been many struggles in our hundred-year history, but right now we've never been in a better spot. We're firing on all eight cylinders."

Originally published in *Family Business*, www.familybusinessmagazine.com

Chapter 32

Pay Attention To Attention

"Don't be afraid to try unconventional tactics to get attention"

The sounds of a baby crying or a telephone ringing are said to be impossible to ignore. Can the same be said about your advertising?

Getting your prospective customer's attention is the crucial first function of every ad, whether it be in print, broadcast, or on the side of your delivery truck. As advertising giant Bill Bernbach said, "If your advertising goes unnoticed, everything else is academic." If they don't even read it, they can't respond to it.

You want your advertising to stand out from the sea of background noise and forest of pictures and text that your prospective customers inhabit. That means your ads or commercials have to contrast with that environment in some way. Camouflage works because it looks like the world around it. Your advertising needs to do just the opposite. It needs to be anti-camo, like a hunter's orange vest.

People pay attention to the unusual and the unexpected. A magazine ad picturing magnificently lush grass with the headline "Ugly lawn" will jolt the reader's expectations and draw them into the body copy for an explanation. Such an attention-getting device also serves another purpose by reinforcing the selling points of the copy. When the reader learns that the lawn is "ugly" to white grubs, mole crickets, and sod webworms because the homeowner applied Product X, the ad does it's job. As another advertising legend, David Ogilvy, once wrote, "When you advertise fire-extinguishers, open with the fire."

Literally shouting "Hey you!" is one way to grab notice. It's blunt, it's simple, and it works pretty well for two reasons. The first is that it uses "hey," a common word instantly and unambiguously recognized as a demand for attention. The second is that it addresses the most important person in the universe, you. If someone is going to say something about you, your first inclination is to want to hear it.

There's nothing wrong with the blunt direct approach, either, as long as it accomplishes the task at hand without undermining the rest of your ad's message. If your attention-getting device isn't related to your selling points, it can make the viewer or reader feel deceived, which is no way to start a relationship. Screaming "Look out!" will cause heads to snap around immediately, but the people with the twisted necks will be angry when they find out there's no danger coming their way.

Pictures and words

Each advertising medium has its own repertoire of techniques to help you capture the prospective customer's attention. In print ads, headlines and illustrations help pull the reader in. The Newspaper Association of America, citing a study they commissioned by Roper Starch Worldwide, says that showing the product attracts readers 13% more than not showing the product. Multi-product visuals in ads are 25% more likely to attract readers and, in ads where three-quarters of the space is devoted to illustrations, recall rates improve by 50%. Using full color in an ad increases its recall by 20% over black and white.

Not surprisingly, the NAA reports that ad size relates to readership, with full page ads recalled 40% more often than quarter-page ads. Interestingly, though, even small six inch ads are recalled 59% as often as a full-page. In other words, buy only as much space as you need to show off what you want to sell. Don't spend money on space simply to get attention, since a good headline with an arresting illustration will do the job just as well.

Pictures aren't everything, though. At one time, David Ogilvy estimated that five times more people read the headline than read the body copy in a print ad, so attention to the big, bold type at the top of the ad pays off, too. After all, it's the job of the headline to make the reader want to continue looking at the rest of the ad. There are many standard headline-writing techniques you can use. Making it read like a news bulletin is one. Another is to offer "congratulations, you've won" and entice the reader to dig deeper to discover the prize. And don't underestimate the power of the ever-popular word "free" to motivate someone to try to learn more. Just make sure when using come-ons like these that they are legitimate; a deceived reader makes a lousy customer.

Billboards and other forms of outdoor advertising fail miserably without some sort of attention-getter because they lack editorial context to attract the reader or viewer in the first place. Probably the single most important feature of an outdoor attention-getter is simplicity. It can't be subtle; it can't be bland; it has to work right away. And, to be truly effective, the attention-getting device needs to express the prime selling point as well. Lilly-Miller Garden Grow's OBIE-winning billboard that said "Grass Hasn't Been This Good Since The Sixties" comes to mind as a good example.

Radio and TV

Many of the same principles apply to getting attention in radio. Instead of pictures, though, you use sound effects, music, and high-impact copy. Regardless of the methods you use, it's essential that your radio commercial sound different from the programming on the station on which it's playing, since radio is often in the background of the listener's consciousness to start with. If you're advertising on a talk station, use music. If you're running on a country music station, try spots that sound like news. Whatever you do, make sure it doesn't just blend in with the sound of the station.

Television advertising presents a dilemma. On the one hand, it's hard to get the viewer's attention because of the cluttered ad environment. On the other, it's easy because you have so many different and effective tools to use. You not only have an illustration, it's in color and you can make it move. And, with today's digital effects technology, you can make it jump, jiggle, dance, or morph in very unexpected and unusual ways. You get to use sound effects, music, and dialogue, too.

And television allows you to use a spokesperson, too, which opens up a whole realm of out-of-the-ordinary characters, crazy consumers, or memorable mascots. It's hard to imagine anyone who wasn't glued to the set as soon as the Taco Bell Chihuahua first opened his mouth.

Don't be afraid to try unconventional tactics to get attention with your television (or any other) advertising. Sometimes, an offbeat approach pays unexpected dividends. Consider the Orkin Pest Control commercial that used a special-effects-produced cockroach that appeared to crawl across the viewer's television screen. That commercial not only riveted viewer attention, it generated a substantial amount of priceless publicity.

The single most important factor in gaining attention is being different. The crying baby always draws a response--unless it happens to be in the newborn room at the hospital where there are fifteen others crying the same tune. To make your ads work, make them stand out. It pays to pay attention to attention.

Chapter 33

Advertising's Four-Letter Word

"When you tell someone something they already know—
or think they know—they stop listening.
Just ask anyone with teenage children."

Back in the good old days when parents actually corrected their children's behavior, your mother might wash your mouth out with soap if you used certain four-letter words. Today, you should do the same to whomever writes your advertising (even if that's you) if your ads contain the most offensive four-letter word in advertising, "have."

It's scary how often we hear this terrible, nasty word. "We have name brand merchandise." "We have friendly, knowledgeable personnel." "We have the latest equipment." "We have everything from soup to nuts." You don't have to look very far to see how prevalent the have approach is in retail (and other) advertising. Newspaper ads tell readers what the store has with pictures of items with prices next to them. TV spots show pictures of items with prices superimposed on them and an announcer telling the viewer what they are seeing. Radio commercials do the same without the pictures.

Why is it a bad practice to tell the customer what you have? Because that takes up expensive space and time that could be put to much better use giving the customer a reason to do business with you. Good ads don't tell the customer what you have. Instead, they answer the key question, "What's in it for me?" That's an important distinction to make when every advertising dollar needs to produce maximum results.

A reason to buy

Simply telling the customer what you have does not give them a reason to act. It doesn't provide a rationale for buying the items listed. All it does is tell the customer something they probably already know, which is what kinds of merchandise and services you offer. When you tell someone something they already know—or think they know—they stop listening. Just ask anyone with teenage children. When customers stop listening to your advertising, it's money down the drain.

Let's face it, if your sign says "speed shop," for example, most people know that you sell and install auto performance products. This goes double for anyone who has ever been in your shop or one like it. They've seen what you have with their own eyes and aren't learning anything new from your ads. The lack of worthwhile information in advertising is one of the main reasons people tune it out and why so much advertising doesn't produce results.

Communications expert Dorothy Leeds says that every customer listens to their own personal radio station, called WII-FM. That stands for "What's In It For Me." Good advertising is like a song that gets played often on that radio station. So stop using that four letter word "have" and start telling the customer what you're going to do for them. Give them a reason to get in their SUV, drive to your shop, and open their wallet. Tell them how they will benefit from doing business with you.

Benefits vs. features

Learning how to demonstrate product benefits instead of features is one of the most important skills a salesperson can master. The same holds true for good advertising. A benefit is something that satisfies one or more of the customer's needs. A feature is simply a component of the product. A mediocre salesperson will spend the customer's time telling them the pneumatic jack has an ergonomic handle but never tell them that purchasing this particular piece of equipment will ease the pain in their back. The first is a feature, the second is a benefit. People don't buy features and products; they buy benefits.

This is particularly true of new-to-the-market customers, who may not be fully educated about what a particular type of product can do for them. If, for example, a "newbie" reads your ad that simply says you "have" both wet and dry sump oil systems, he or she may not know they can eliminate blowing oil and increase horsepower, so they ignore it. Even though they might be good prospects for the product, you'll never know because they won't respond to the ad. It's easy to assume that your customers know as much about what a product does as you do, but that's an expensive assumption.

Prices are features too

Keep in mind that prices in your ads are nothing more than features of the items you're selling. And like other features, prices don't mean much out of context. If the customer doesn't know whether the price you're offering is a good one, they have to do some research to find out. And that research may include a visit to your competitor—not usually a desired advertising result.

So the same principle holds true: Don't just tell the customer how much it costs; tell them what benefit that price delivers. Instead of saying "All gloves are 50% off," tell the customer to "Buy two for the price of one." Or, even better, "Protect your hands two times for the price of once."

Also look for "we have" in disguise. Sometimes it masquerades as phrases like "we offer" or "we carry" or "we sell." It takes a little more mental effort to turn your features into benefits, but the results make it very worthwhile.

There are two exceptions to the "have" rule. The first is when you want to announce something new or exclusive—and even then a benefit should be included: "We have just added a new selection of magnetic filters to protect the machined surfaces in your engine." It doesn't hurt anything to add the benefit to the announcement and it will definitely improve the ad's response from prospective customers to whom the technology is new.

The second exception is in the Yellow Pages. Customers usually use this medium to find specific items, so you do need to tell them you have what they're looking for. These customers are generally knowledgeable about what they need and want—they're just looking for a source. That's also why it's a good idea to spread your listings among many headings—you increase the chance of reaching someone looking for a specific type of product or service.

Aside from these specific exceptions, try to concentrate on telling the customer what you're going to do for them. As Leo Burnet, one of the world's most successful advertising practitioners, said, "Good advertising does not just circulate information. It penetrates the public mind with desires and belief."

From "Have" to "What's in it for me?"

How do you apply this concept to your ads? Look for every use of the word have (or its equivalent) and turn it into a benefit instead. Here are some examples of translating the features your store has into the benefits the customer receives from spending money there.

Feature: We have a huge selection of brand-name merchandise

Benefit: You'll find exactly what you want in our huge selection from manufacturers you trust.

Feature: We provide fast shipping

Benefit: When you need it, you need it NOW! That's why we offer same-day shipping.

Feature: Our personnel have 100 years of combined experience.

Benefit: You can trust our expert advice based on 100 years of combined experience.

Feature: We offer a one-year guarantee.

Benefit: You can rest easy knowing that your purchase is backed up by our one-year guarantee.

So look at your ads the way your mother listened to your language. Improve your vocabulary—and your advertising response—by doing away with that particularly nasty four-letter word, "have."

Chapter 34

Just A Little Reminder

"Advertising works more like a directional arrow.
It tells the customer where to go to get something
once they've decided they need it."

Some of us occasionally have what are known as senior moments. A name, a phone number, where we parked our car, some bit of information we have known in the past suddenly disappears and we're left with a blank. You can only hope your customers never have a senior moment when it comes time to place an order for what you sell.

The best defense against that unfortunate event (and a few others) is to consistently use a slogan, a jingle, a distinctive graphic or some other memory aid in all of your marketing efforts. This mnemonic device—or memory trigger—serves a very simple but crucial purpose: It reminds the customer where to go when the urge to buy arises.

Advertising doesn't create market demand. Your ad doesn't make the customer suddenly need your product or service. It may help them recognize or define a desire that already exists, but it doesn't generate it in the first place. Instead, advertising works more like a directional arrow. It tells the customer where to go to get something once they've decided they need it. A memory device in your advertising is what makes the process work.

Nearly everyone instantly recognizes the products associated with some of the great slogans. Fill in these blanks:

You're in good hands with _____ (a.)

How do you spell relief? __ __ __ __ __ __ __ (b.)

_____. It's everywhere you want to be (c.)

Like a good neighbor, _____ is there (d.)

All of these slogans share some key elements that have made them effective memory devices:

- They illustrate the prime benefit the customer receives from the product.

- They include the product or company name, which ties the benefit to the purchase.

- They're short, which makes them easy to remember.

The first element—expressing the prime benefit—is particularly important. Let's say you sell gift baskets. Consumers don't buy such baskets to satisfy some primal need to own pretty containers filled with shredded paper and fancy food items. They buy them because the basket does something for them. It demonstrates their appreciation for an employee's performance. It brings some happiness into a loved one's life. It mends a fence with an unhappy customer.

A good advertising memory device tells the consumer who feels one of these needs how it can be satisfied. When the customer notices a friend's anniversary in her date book, a good memory device will complete the equation: gift = XYZ Gift Baskets.

Slogans aren't all

Slogans aren't the only memory devices that perform this function. Jingles are used very effectively on radio or TV. In fact, one of the slogans above serves double duty as the lyrics for the company's jingle. Graphic elements can trigger consumer memory, too. One that comes quickly to mind is Apple Computer's apple with a bite out of it. The unspoken but clear benefit conveyed is that the product delivers a piece of the tree of knowledge. The item itself, of course, shouts the company name—in any language!

Can your ads have an effective memory device? Absolutely. But before you start jotting down song lyrics, be sure to take time to identify the prime benefit your customers want. Is it convenience, selection, uniqueness? How about value, quality, or service? Once you've established this, go on to the next step, which is coming up with the phrase, song, or visual to express it.

Do it right

Go back for a moment to the examples. Did you notice what they didn't have? There was no comedy or humor, no rhyming words, and no puns or word plays. It's not that these features can't be used. It's just that they are very difficult to use well. They also have a short life—the consumer may think the pun is very clever the first twelve times they hear it, but grow to hate it and to block it out by the twentieth. Great ad memory devices last a long time; one example above was first used in 1950! But do you remember the products associated with these zingers?

The best seat in the house. _____ (e.)

Sight for soaring eyes. _____(f.)

These clever slogans failed the ultimate test of a good memory device: they couldn't stand repeated exposure over time. A good memory trigger gets used everywhere over and over again. In every ad, brochure, or business card. On every piece of paper from customer invoices to cash register tapes. On every delivery van, sign, and billboard. On price tags, packaging, and P.O.P. displays. If you use a jingle, play it along with the background music in your store. In other words, expose it everywhere all the time.

If you use a memory trigger successfully, it will deliver your marketing message to the consumer in the ultimate medium at the perfect time: in their brain when they want to buy.

How's your memory?

(a) Allstate

(b) Rolaids

(c) VISA

(d) State Farm

(e) Jockey Underwear

(f) TWA

Chapter 35
Should Price Be In The Picture?

"There's generally no reason to use price advertising since few purchase decisions are made on that basis."

Should you put prices in your advertising? Only if you want to drive away new customers.

Why, then, do so many ads seem to center on low prices? Because we tend to exaggerate the importance of pricing based subjectively on our experiences with customers. Most customers seem to object to our price in some way (regardless of what it is), so we assume that price must be the major factor in their purchase decision. We stick a price in the ad because we think that's what the customer wants.

We also lean on price advertising many times because we don't know what else to put in our ads. We forget that our customers are not buying a commodity. If you run a photography studio, for example, they're buying a unique and highly personal service that produces a product with great emotional value. It's literally impossible to put a price on a memory.

Prices are a deterrent to a purchase, not a reason for making it. That's because there are only two kinds of new customers; those who can't afford your price and those who think there must be something wrong with your service if the price is that low. An advertised price drives both away. Those who don't have the ability to pay are filtered out by the price in your ad, although that may actually be a desirable result.

The damage comes, of course, from the customer who can afford you but interprets your price advertising as a clue to the quality of your work. It's what they've been conditioned to think by the thousands of ads they are exposed to every day. Consider some examples: Who advertises price, Kia or BMW? Timex or Rolex? Motel 6 or Marriott? Which brand more closely resembles the image you want to project? Or delivers the profit margins you want to achieve?

Price-driven customers?

There's generally no reason to use price advertising in the first place since few purchase decisions are made solely on that basis. Consider the photographer: with the average wedding costing nearly $20,000, there's not much scrimping going on in the marketplace. Negotiation, yes—but price shopping, less than you think. The stereotypical struggling newlywed couple has nearly disappeared. Bridal Faire reports that the combined income of 38% of newlyweds is $60-80,000; 53% earn $80-100,000 and another 9% bring in $100,000 or more! These consumers may shop frugally but they expect to—and will—pay for quality service.

When to advertise price

Strangely enough, you can use price advertising to achieve a very specific goal: to generate more business from your previous customers. They already know you do high quality work so the price ad they see doesn't influence their thinking about you. Since they have information other than the price of your work to guide them about the quality they get when they turn to you, they can be safely approached with a price promotion.

The trick is to make sure your previous customers are the only ones who see the price ad, since its exposure to new customers will work against you. That makes direct mail, private sales, and other such highly targeted promotional tactics the best vehicle for price advertising.

The new customer hasn't experienced your service and has to draw conclusions about the quality of your work based almost entirely on your advertising. Since prices tend to dominate ads, the negative price vs. quality effect is magnified in the prospect's mind.

Advertising can be a highly effective way to send a message to your customers and prospects. Just be sure that the message is the one you want to send.

Chapter 36

Four Rules For Buying Advertising

"You really shouldn't hide in the back
when a media salesperson comes into your business."

Paying your advertising bill is like sending in your kid's college tuition; you know you have to do it but you're not sure what you're getting out of it. Or, as John Wanamaker supposedly said, "I know half the money I spend on advertising is wasted, but I can never find out which half."

Buying advertising time and space from the local media doesn't have to be quite so mysterious. Advertising results can never be guaranteed, but you can be much more certain that your media investment pays off if you follow a few simple rules:

Rule One: Target the customer

Only buy media that reaches your target customer. This sounds obvious, yet it is the rule most often violated by retail and other small business advertisers because media salespeople specialize in talking about big numbers like circulation and listeners and how many spots are in their package. But the total circulation of the newspaper, the total viewership of the local TV stations, or the total number of eyeballs driving past a billboard are poor indicators of how well they reach your particular target customer. If your most profitable customer is a guy aged 35-54 who owns a bicycle and lives within a twenty-five-mile radius of your bike shop, the number of them exposed to your ads is the only number that counts.

Your media reps should provide that information to you since most of them subscribe to ratings and research services that provide the data. They may not have audience data that includes bicycle ownership, but they should have info on sex, age, and location of their viewers, readers, or listeners. If the rep says they don't have that information, it's likely that the outlet's audience is so small that they're not worth messing with anyway. Buying advertising without audience data is like buying a mutual fund from a broker who won't tell you whether it holds stocks, bonds, or tulip bulb options; you might get lucky, but the odds are against you.

When you request the information, though, it's possible that a quick-thinking media rep will tell you that his or her paper or station reaches almost 100% of the market, so your target customer is covered. That argument may be true on the face of it, but you still need a hard number of target customers reached so that you can follow...

Rule Two: Calculate efficiency

Check the cost efficiency to reach your target customer. Generally speaking, the greater the total circulation of any medium, the higher their rates. This may still give them an apparently cheaper cost-per-thousand (a standard measure of cost efficiency determined by dividing the cost of the ad or spot by the number of readers or viewers in thousands) but may not make them the most cost efficient way to reach your best customer. Here's a simplified example:

The Weekly Perspirer charges $500 for an ad that is read by 20,000 people, of whom 4,000 are your target customers. Their total cost-per-thousand is $500 divided by 20, or $25, but the cost to reach a thousand target customers is $500 divided by 4, or $125. Station KGRO-TV, however, has a $500 spot package reaching a smaller total audience of 15,000 people ($33 per thousand), of whom 5,000 are your target customers. That's more than the newspaper's 4,000 target customers. That means the TV station delivers a thousand target customers for $100—and are the better buy on this basis.

It's sometimes said that figures lie and liars figure and that certainly holds true for buying media. It is very easy to start comparing apples to kumquats if you don't consider a few other factors. Geography is one. A given newspaper reader or radio listener may fit every one of your target customer criteria but happen to live forty miles away—they should probably be excluded from your calculations unless you normally draw customers from that distance.

Another little detail to look for is how many times each person in the audience is counted. Radio, TV, and cable are particularly fond of quoting "gross reach," which is simply the sum of the audiences delivered by every spot in the schedule. But that means the guy who watches the six o'clock news and then tunes in again for Gasoline Alley Revisted is counted twice. You need to ask them to provide net reach data.

Finally, just to make your life less complicated, ask for all information in thousands, not percentages. A rating is a specific media measurement—not a generic term. It is defined as the size of the audience expressed as a percentage of the audience universe. Since the audience universe can vary from medium to medium (cable ratings are often a percentage of the number of subscribing homes, for example, whereas broadcast TV ratings are usually percentages of a specific geographic area which may in turn be a different area from that used by a radio station), you need absolute audience figures to make true comparisons.

Rule Three: Timing is everything

Advertise most when the target customers are buying. As Woody Allen said, "Ninety percent of success if being there." Advertising research has shown that customers tend to remember and act on the most recent ad they've seen when they get ready to make a purchase. Conversely, they tend to ignore ads if they are not in the market for that product at that time. If you bought a new car last month, for example, you probably started tuning out the endless car commercials in the local news on TV the day you took delivery. When you're shopping for a car, though, you see every one of them.

What does this mean for your ad budget? It means there's no point in spending money to promote much of anything in January if you run a bike shop and the bike racing season in your market doesn't start until May. Instead, concentrate your spending during the buying season—and maintain it throughout the period. Which brings us to...

Rule Four: Concentrate

Don't spread too thin. It's generally wiser to concentrate your spending in a few places than to spread it among multiple outlets. For one thing, the more you spend with any one medium, the better the deal you'll get, and, for another, the more consistent your advertising, the better the odds that the customer will see it at the right time.

That's not to say that you should put all your eggs in one basket. Instead, a good plan is to start with your number one media choice based on the above criteria and buy enough exposure to reach most—but not more than all—of the target customers it delivers every week, then buy the number two choice up to that level, followed by the third, fourth, etc. until the entire budget is committed. This is a simplistic approach but it pretty much ensures the most efficient and effective use of your ad dollars.

It's always a great temptation, but you really shouldn't hide in the back when a media salesperson comes into your business. If you make them help you follow these four rules, you'll find that your advertising dollar goes a lot further and produces much stronger results.

Chapter 37

Case Study:

Lehman's Hardware

"The Lehman family of Ohio sells
butter churns and washboards—via the Internet."

Lehman's Hardware and Appliance in Kidron, Ohio—one of the last retailers of butter churns in America—faces some issues today. But the biggest problem at the 50-year-old family company isn't what you might expect. Lehman family members aren't struggling to avoid the fate of the fabled buggy-whip manufacturer. Their challenge is how to manage their company's double-digit growth.

As Lehman's enters its second half-century, the purveyor of low-tech items like hand-cranked blenders and kerosene-powered incubators is also dealing with succession planning, management control, and balancing the demands of its traditional customer base—local Amish farmers—with an ever-growing crush of tourists sticking their fingers into the lanterns on display to see if the flames are real.

The family members who run the company take pride in having built an operation with annual sales that exceed $10 million from what founder Jay Lehman describes as an old, run-down country hardware store that he bought in 1955 at the age of 26. They are noticeably excited about what the future holds as the second generation takes over and works to preserve the company for the third. There's a steadiness about the Lehmans that comes from their rock-solid religious beliefs and strong sense of values.

"I'm far from perfect, but my faith has allowed me to see how others feel," says second-generation president Galen Lehman, 44. "Trying to make sure employees have a fair and complete benefits package. Trying to make sure that customers don't walk out feeling taken advantage of. It's easier in a family-owned business, where you know that the other people in management share your views."

Preserving the past

Back in 1955, Jay Lehman, who had left school in the tenth grade, abandoned plans to look for a job when he found a one-room store in Kidron—an hour south of Cleveland—in the midst of the nation's largest Amish community, where profound religious faith dictates self-reliance and a quiet, non-technical lifestyle. The new young storekeeper—a member of the Mennonite faith, a Christian sect from which the Amish split three centuries ago—was soon peppered with questions about parts for things like oil stoves and ice boxes.

"Most people would have said, 'You can't get it anymore,'" says Jay's son Galen, who became president in 2002. Instead, Jay searched for vendors to help the Amish preserve their way of life. He found parts for oil stoves in South America and contracted with a local manufacturer to make ice boxes. A unique business was born that today sells what it calls historical technology including apple peelers, broad axes, farm bells, pickle kegs and zinc washboards. The greatest single contributor to sales, Jay reports, is a line of gas-powered refrigerators; the company sold 1,568 of them last year (for about $1,200 each).

The Wall Street Journal, Time magazine, *USA Today*, the *London Telegraph, Business Week* and National Public Radio, among other media outlets, have noted the historical authenticity of Lehman's products.

Lantern-seller to the stars

So have many Hollywood producers. Among the recent movies featuring Lehman's merchandise were *Cold Mountain* with Nicole Kidman, *Open Range* with Kevin Costner and *Pirates of the Caribbean* with Johnny Depp. The company also served as historical technology consultants for the PBS series *Frontier House.*

Lehman's global outreach began in 1960, when Jay answered the call of the Mennonite Central Committee and took his wife Ella Mae (who died in 1999) and young family to Africa. Jay's brother Dave, now 68, ran the little Ohio hardware store, while Jay operated a travel agency for missionaries in Africa for 12 years.

"While Dad was overseas, he realized that missionaries and others lived a lot like the Amish because they had to live a life off of the power grid," says Jay's and Ella Mae's daughter Glenda Lehman Ervin, 42, who was born in what is now the Congo and today serves as Lehman's VP. "That's one reason we ship products all over the world."

There are literally thousands of missionaries in Africa, as well as people who live on islands and in remote areas and in the mountains, Jay explains. These customers aren't necessarily hermits who've taken vows of poverty, either. For example, many thousand-plus-acre ranches have limited electrical service, and their owners are steady Lehman's customers.

Another key market is the burgeoning tourist trade. Travelers are drawn by nostalgic yearnings to the no-longer-little hardware store. Some 500,000 of them annually meander wide-eyed through the maze of eight interconnected additions. Says Glenda, "I can't tell you how many times we hear, 'I haven't seen one of these since ...'" Among the big tourist attractions are the store's museum-quality antiques, including a 1921 Model T and a 1912 Rumley Oil Pull Tractor. Tourists are wonderful customers, the Lehmans say, but the staff must make sure the tourists treat the regular

Amish customers with respect, reminding them to refrain from taking pictures of the Amish as if they were characters in an amusement park.

Though Galen estimates that the Amish now account for only about 10% of sales, the Lehmans have not turned their backs on this market. They operate another, smaller store in nearby Mt. Hope, Ohio, called Mt. Hope Hardware, that caters primarily to Amish customers by carrying standard items like nails and paint and foregoing the tourist-oriented merchandise like sock monkeys. The Lehmans also do business with Amish vendors. One Amish-made item, a wooden wheelbarrow, flew off the shelves after Time magazine mentioned it in an article during the 2004 holiday shopping season.

Classic products advertised the modern way

Lehman's traditional wares gained new popularity during periods of national crisis (or potential crisis). "During the oil embargo of the late '70s, our business really started booming," Jay recalls. "All at once, everybody wanted to buy wood-burning stoves."

In late 1999, as the fear of large-scale Y2K computer crashes mounted, demand for Lehman's eclectic selection of water purifiers, grain mills and butchering supplies drove sales through the roof. "Y2K really put us on the map," Jay says. Orders during this period zoomed to 3,500 per week from an average of 400 per week in the year before.

Sales rose again after the terrorist attacks of Sept. 11, 2001. "What we've seen since 9/11, sadly enough, is that people in cities are looking at kerosene heaters, oil lamps, hand-cranked radios," Glenda says. "In a post-9/11 world, everyone fears the worst." Family members say they try to act according to their family values when assisting such customers. "We try never to capitalize on people's fears," Glenda says. "If somebody in Florida says they need a wood-heating stove, we tell them, 'That may not be something you need to invest your money in.'"

The Lehmans transformed their company in response to the crush of Y2K customers. Galen decided they needed a more effective website to take some of the pressure off the phones. Today, www.lehmans.com offers thousands of items, as well as a live chat feature that enables visitors to receive near-instant answers to their questions. Today half of the company's sales are consummated by mail, and the website is close to producing more sales than the 200,000-copy print catalog. The company recently purchased a 100,000-square-foot former lawnmower manufacturing plant and is converting it into a mail-order facility and corporate offices.

"It's sort of ironic that we cater to people who don't like electricity, but our business is run more and more by the web, and e-mail, and things like that," Jay observes.

Indeed, the Internet is a lifeline for many of Lehman's customers. "Missionaries often go to a cyber-café," Glenda explains. "We got an e-mail from a doctor in East Africa thanking us for our water filters because he uses them to purify postoperative I-V solutions."

Lehman's is now implementing a computerized storewide inventory control system, and Galen worries about how his 100-person work force will handle it. "We have people on staff who know how to churn butter and we have people who know how to grind meat," he says, "but those skills aren't necessarily compatible with the computerized world. One of the challenges for us is to find a way to use technology that preserves the values that we stand for."

Building on beliefs

The Lehmans say their religion shapes the business every day. "If anyone has a serious faith," Galen asserts, "it has to cover everything they do."

Glenda says their faith has helped them weather some typical family business storms. "One of the things that is very common in the Mennonite culture is conflict avoidance," she notes. "We have had several times when something could potentially take on a negative twist, and we've talked about it early and openly." One such issue arose when Glenda joined the company eight years ago after a career in corporate communications with a Fortune 200 company. Family discussions made it clear that Galen was to be in charge and Glenda's role would be equal to that of any of the other, non-family department head.

Galen says working with his father and sister is a huge plus because there is a sense of trust with family members that you can't get any other way. He points out, "You know how they'll react in given situations, which enhances that sense of trust."

Despite their closeness, Galen says, the family strives to ensure that family issues don't affect their working relationships. "What we've done is to work very hard to compartmentalize our lives into the business side and the family side," he says. "To make sure the family remains strong, we have an annual meeting. At times we've brought in outside consultants with expertise in family business to put us through workshops."

Adds Glenda, "We determined a long time ago that the family members were here to run the business; the business was not here to support the family."

Practicing what they preach

Glenda Lehman Ervin and her young family don't just talk about historically accurate, environmentally friendly living. They are designing a new home, currently under construction, based on these principles. Using local multigenerational family-owned Amish contractors and local materials, the Ervins are building a 4,500-square-foot home that will be equipped primarily with goods from Lehman's and furnished with pieces made by local craftsmen.

Glenda says she and her husband, Scott, 43, a senior estimator for a large commercial construction company in Cleveland, are using the construction project to show their children how to close the loop when it comes to the environment. They preserved as many trees as possible on the building site, for example, but her husband and son cut the felled timber into stove wood that they will use to heat the new home.

The generational transfer at Lehman's seems well on its way to completion. Beginning about five years ago, Jay started delegating more responsibility to Galen. He also told everyone else in the family what was going to happen. They all own shares in the S Corporation, but Galen now has voting control. "Dad's always felt pretty strongly that should be vested in one person," Galen says, "to prevent the kind of family blowups that often happen after the founder is out of the picture. He's also worked at explaining the way it's structured to everybody in the family while he's still here."

Galen and Glenda each have two children. The eldest is only 15, so decisions about the third generation are a little premature. They hope their children will choose to carry on, but the operative word is choose, according to both of them. Glenda is optimistic, though. She says her nine-year-old son has already drawn up blueprints for a store addition that will feature model trains—non-electric, of course.

Originally published in *Family Business*, www.familybusinessmagazine.com

Section Three

Twenty-three Promotions
And Ad Campaigns
You Can Use

About These Marketing Ideas

As I hope you've concluded, this book is short on theory and long on successful practice. It's not a textbook about "why," it's a description of "how." This section in particular is about specific advertising ideas you can use right away. They are promotional advertising campaigns to build profitable sales for the small business.

These particular promotion ideas were collected during my work in media sales, consulting, and training. Each one was developed to fulfill the needs of an actual client. They've been tested, refined, and re-tested in the real world by local businesses from coast to coast. I can't honestly say that I created every detail of every one of these ideas. Many of them were hatched in brainstorming sessions that I led as part of my training programs. As such, they were the result of collaboration with hundreds of salespeople and their managers. The brainstorming sessions have always been one of the most popular segments of my courses—with both the participants and with me.

I also served as sort of a "Typhoid Mary" of promotion ideas, carrying the germ of the ideas from market to market as I worked with various clients. This part of the process did two things: it eliminated the less-than-successful ideas and it honed the best ones to a sharp edge. These promotion ideas represent the best of the best selected through that ruthless process.

Each promotion idea includes a description of the market situation in which it works best, a step-by-step outline for executing it, and examples of what types of businesses have used it and how they've made it successful.

You'll also find some helpful do's and don'ts and some insider tips on how to work with media reps and other vendors to get what you need without paying more than you should.

Done right, every one of these promotions will be successful because:

- The customer hears about it—through advertising, news coverage, or word of mouth.

- The customer remembers it—because it's different from what everyone else is doing.

- The customer likes it—because it offers benefits and value that appeals to them.

Like everything else a manager does, designing and executing promotions and ad campaigns take a little extra work and usually entail spending some money. But, as you'll find as you examine these ideas, you're not necessarily alone—even when it comes to paying for your promotion. You can look for help in that department from two sources, vendors and the media itself.

Depending on the promotion, of course, many vendors will kick in a little extra merchandising money if their products can have a featured position in the promotion. Some of these advertising ideas lend themselves to multiple vendor participation, which can significantly lower the cost. The local media may also add some support, too, in return for a share of the budget to advertise some of these promotions. Theirs may come in the form of an offer to barter extra ad time for prizes or free promotional announcements that are added to your schedule in return for sponsorship participation. In either case, the best way to find out what the vendors and media will do for you is to describe your idea and see what kind of support they offer. I suggest beginning the negotiations without asking for something specific. You might be very pleasantly surprised at what they come up with on their own.

The most important thing to do as you consider these advertising ideas is to keep an open mind. Not every one of them will be right for your company, but some variation or off-shoot may be just what you need to pump up your sales in the short term or build your customer base for the long.

So use these ideas as starting points. Give one you like to one of your media vendors or your ad agency (if you have one) and ask them to give you a proposal for the way they would do it. You and I don't have a monopoly on good ideas and their knowledge of your business, the local market area, and their general expertise can make them excellent partners.

Don't forget to look inside your business, too. Just about any of these ideas makes a great starter for a staff brainstorming session. Pass one around and solicit comments on how you can make it better. Who knows, you may have a budding advertising genius selling ties in the men's department. A side benefit to this approach is that people give greater support to a plan they've helped develop.

Even if you never use a single one of these specific ideas, though, reading about them will help spark some ideas of your own. Adopt the strategies and modify the tactics to make your cash register ring.

Idea 1

The Distance Discount

Has your business been around for many years? So long that everybody in town knows you're there and knows what you sell? That's great, but it also has a downside. Sometimes, it means you've captured as much of your local market as can get without a major change in your business strategy.

Change is often good, but it may endanger your relationship with your current customers. The solution? Expand your market area. If you sell higher-ticket items, potential customers may be willing to drive some distance to buy from you. That means you can grow your sales by bringing in more customers from out of town.

As with all promotions, you need to do two things to accomplish this goal:

1. Let the target customer know about your opportunity

2. Give them a reason to take advantage of it.

A good way to do this is to offer the Distance Discount. The concept is simple: the farther a customer drives to your store, the bigger the discount they receive.

Structure this promotion to last three months, which is long enough to have the desired effect without running so long that the novelty value of the offer wears off. It's highly repeatable, though, so you could use it once every year to spur sales in a slow period or to take advantage of regional themes or events (see the variations that follow later in this chapter).

We're going to use a car dealer as our prototype, but the concept will apply equally well to furniture or appliances, boats and RV's, or any other high-ticket merchandise for which people are willing to spend some time shopping. If you sell items that require installation or maintenance that you provide, however, you might want to be cautious about setting the parameters.

Week 1

In the first week of the promotion, your ads should tease potential customers by warning them to not buy a car (or appliance, or furniture, etc.) until next week, when you're going to unveil a revolutionary discount plan.

These ads can be short, but the media exposure must be heavy. They're teasers designed to get the attention of prospects in the market today for your type of product. And, since you want to create a little air of mystery, you shouldn't give any details about the promotion. The ads don't need to be fancy but they do need to have your name and location. Not your address—just your town or city.

Weeks 2-5

Beginning in the second week, advertise the distance discount details. Your ads should tell customers to come in and make their best deal with you—negotiating their trade-in, finance terms, factory rebates, etc. Be sure to point out that they're already saving on your normally low prices. Then instruct them to tell you where they live. For each mile they've come to buy from you, they'll get an additional $1.00 off the price of their new car.

All they need is some proof of residence to establish the amount of their discount. A driver's license or utility bill will do. You can use an area road map to calculate the distance or have it done for you by any of the mapping software programs available online.

Promote the distance discount in this way for four weeks. The goal of this phase of the promotion is to establish the concept in the prospect's mind. This is the learning stage, although it should also produce a growing swell of sales.

Weeks 6-9

For the following four weeks, change the copy to emphasize the benefits of the offer rather then the details. Here's what the customer gets when they take advantage of the distance discount:

- Top quality merchandise
- Backed by your reputation
- Real, significant savings

It's going to be tempting to devote most of the ad to the discount offer. Keep in mind, though, that low price by itself is not a reason to buy. The customer has to believe that the value they're receiving—the benefits they'll get from owning the product itself—are worth purchasing. The current low price just gives them a reason to buy now from you.

A good basic guideline for this phase would be to devote fifty percent of the ad to product benefits and fifty percent to the discount.

Weeks 10-13

The final four weeks raises the excitement level for the customers—and for your staff. Close the promotion by offering the Double Distance Discount—but only for customers who buy before the end date.

The Double Distance Discount is just what the name describes: you'll give $2 off the purchase price instead of $1 for each mile traveled by the customer to your store. The same pricing rules and procedures apply.

Now's the time to swing the emphasis of the ad copy more toward the price appeal. But you'll also want to pound home the deadline. Now's the time to move those fence-sitters in your direction by creating a sense of urgency. So change the copy element mix to 25% product benefits, 50% price, and 25% deadline.

And when the promotion's over, it's over. As soon as the deadline arrives, stop the ads, remove the signage, and instruct your staff to politely tell customers that the discount ended yesterday. They'll have the customer in front of them, though, so they still have an opportunity to make a sale based on product benefits and value.

Some do's and don'ts

I'm sure you've noticed that there's a potentially fatal flaw in the Distance Discount. Since you're offering a specific dollar rate with a theoretically unlimited total, you could conceivably end up selling the merchandise below cost. Someone could show you a driver's license from Hong Kong, for example, and demand their $12,000 discount!

All you need to prevent bankruptcy is a simple limit disclaimer. You can set a limit on the discount total—$500 for instance—without reducing the impact of the offer. Just make sure that the limit, like the discount itself, is a specific dollar figure and never a percent off. To today's jaded consumer, dollars are tangible—percentages are suspect.

Alternative tactics

You can also use the Distance Discount in some other ways. Let's say that a competitor in a nearby town changes his business in some way that gives you an opening to go after his customers. You can easily specify that customers from his zip code get the discount, for example.

Or maybe there's an event in your target town like a Founder's Day celebration or Annual Street Fair. You can offer the discount to residents of that town as a tie-in to the event.

Watch for newsworthy happenings out of town, too. What if a neighboring community's high school football team won the state championship? That would be a great time to offer those residents a Booster's Distance Discount.

Choosing your media

The strongest appeal of the Distance Discount is its ability to bring in customers from outside your normal market area. That probably means you'll want to consider advertising media other than the purely local ones you normally use. Your local newspaper is generally distributed in a fairly small geographic area. Cable TV and billboards are likewise limited.

Broadcast media—radio and TV—extend their signals over wider areas, though, and are more efficient for this type of promotion. You just want to be sure that the station(s) you choose have not just coverage but also appeal in the communities you want to reach.

Don't automatically ignore other media, though. You may very well want to choose the local newspaper, cable TV system, or radio station located in a specific neighboring town. Obviously, there may also be copy and/or media rate considerations in your choice.

Idea 2

Neighborhood Bulletin Board

Drawing customers from a wide geographic area with the Distance Discount promotion may not be the strategy for you, though. Location is a key factor in the success of many kinds of businesses. Banks, supermarkets, gas stations, dry cleaners, and even restaurants all depend on a core customer base that lives within a few miles of their facility. The primary reason for this, of course, is ease of access. Small-ticket purchases and frequent transactions are driven by convenience.

The majority of consumer purchase decisions are ultimately made and executed locally—within a few miles of the customer's home. While mail order and online purchasing are growing, they still account for less than half of consumer purchasing. In other words, people prefer to shop where they live.

But there's another factor at work, too. That's trust. Consumers are more likely to trust the businesses with which they're familiar. They know them because they drive by them every day. They know the staff because they deal with them frequently. And if something does go wrong, they can get it corrected without trekking across the country. Proximity breeds trust.

This certainly holds true for the traditional locally-owned neighborhood business—the Mom and Pop grocery store, the corner bakery or hardware store. But it's also a factor for the nationwide chain operator. Those who combine numerous neighborhood-level outlets with a local promotion orientation can be highly successful.

Which is where the Neighborhood Bulletin Board comes in.

Promote your neighborhood

A neighborhood isn't defined just by physical boundaries. Its identity also comes from the activities of the people who live there. What they do together makes them neighbors. To be identified as part of the neighborhood, your business needs to participate in those activities. A great way to do that is to become a primary source of information about upcoming events.

The Neighborhood Bulletin Board is a service you supply and/or sponsor. Through it, you keep your customers and prospects informed about upcoming school fairs, church suppers, neighborhood picnics, etc. This service can be delivered in two basic ways with plenty of alternatives.

Using media

Most local media, particularly TV and radio, have specific features they air to publicize non-profit events. They'll often be called something like the "Community Calendar" and they're simply a listing of events supplied by community organizations. The station considers them public service announcements instead of commercial messages and they're usually put together by the station's community affairs or promotion department.

Such feature programs produce no revenue for the station, so they're usually eager to negotiate a commercial sponsorship of some sort. If this approach is for you, call your ad sales rep and make an offer. Propose a package that includes a sponsor ID, the neighborhood bulletin board feature, and your commercial message. Offer to pay for the commercial message time (at a discounted rate) in return for the station supplying the feature with your ID.

The advantage of this approach is that you don't have to worry about gathering information about events and putting it into presentable form.

The disadvantage is that the items may not be as "local" as you'd like. Broadcast stations serve large geographic areas and typically air information of interest to the widest possible audience. Consequently, the feature you sponsor may publicize events in communities far away from your location. This doesn't help your neighborhood marketing orientation.

One solution to this problem is to specify that the bulletin board contain only items of likely interest to those neighborhoods where you have stores.

Using micro media

The other solution is to stay away from high-reach high-coverage media like radio, TV, and newspapers and use media that pinpoint exactly the area you serve. These can include shoppers, direct mail, and some cable TV systems. To be even more accurate, turn to flyers distributed as door hangers, stuck under windshield wipers, or even handed to passersby on the street.

An extension of this tactic is to enlist neighborhood businesses, schools, churches, and senior centers to post your flyer on their bulletin boards or in their windows. Restaurants in your area may agree to place them on their tables or dry cleaners to attach them to orders as they are picked up. An idea to consider is that you can cut costs (and increase distribution) by sharing sponsorship with one or more non-competitors.

This approach is pretty labor intense. You need sources for information about upcoming events, someone to write and produce the flyers, and arrangements for distribution. Once these are in place, though, it's not actually that big an undertaking. The big advantage of using micro media lies in the way it identifies you as a truly local institution to be trusted and, in fact, rewarded for the service you provide to the neighborhood.

The second advantage is the absolute cost efficiency of the medium. Since you're only distributing your message in the geographic area you serve, you're not paying to reach areas with few if any potential customers. If you choose to use self-distributed flyers, production costs can be limited to the pennies it costs for quick printing.

Overcoming the obstacles

Where are you going to get information about upcoming events? Send a note to every church, school, hospital, social and service club, and other organization you can find asking them to help you help them. Don't forget the scouts, youth sports leagues, PTA's, nursery schools, and fraternal groups in the area.

Give them a contact name and address to send their notices. Send a sample flyer along with your request so they can see the context in which their news will appear. Briefly explain your distribution plans and outline any pertinent deadlines.

Set up a template for your flyer that includes areas both for the event information and your commercial message. You can always use both sides, too, if you need more space. Find a reliable, competitively price printer and you're ready to go.

Distribution will incur some costs just about any way you handle it. Your flyer can be inserted into shoppers or marriage mail packets that are distributed only to the areas you want. This is usually not very expensive, but your flyer will be included with many other pieces and stands a good chance of being overlooked.

You may be able to arrange for door-to-door distribution by a local youth group in return for a donation and exposure for their events. There are also companies who provide this type of service for a fee.

If you can arrange for display of your flyer in area stores, meeting halls, and other facilities, consider faxing or emailing it to them to speed delivery at little cost. You can either mail or hand-deliver to restaurants and other places that need flyers in quantity.

There's obviously a large amount of work involved in establishing the Neighborhood Bulletin Board. The rewards are large, too, though. You'll create goodwill, wrap your commercial message in a customer-friendly presentation, and build the kind of reputation that brings customers back time after time.

Idea 3

Satisfied Neighbors

Here's a multiple choice quiz: Which one of these people is most trustworthy?

- A lawyer
- A car salesman
- A politician
- Your neighbor

Not too tough to choose, is it? If the trustworthiness of your advertising voice is important to your business, consider building your ad campaign around unpaid testimonials from satisfied neighbors of your customers.

This approach works for many reasons. For one thing, "real" people are perceived as more objective than professional pitchmen because they aren't being paid to endorse the store, product or service. For another, they're like you and me, therefore we not only identify with them but believe that what pleases them will please us, too. Generally, people in like circumstances tend to support each other, so you'll believe your neighbor has your best interests at heart when he or she makes a recommendation.

It's all about credibility as demonstrated by another quiz question: Which movie would you be most likely to see, the one with the loudest commercials or the one your neighbor saw last night and really liked?

Having trustworthy spokespeople isn't important just to banks. Almost every type of business could benefit from increasing the credibility of their advertising. A few that come immediately to mind, of course, are car dealers, stockbrokers, or anyone in health care. Some of these businesses have a credibility problem to begin with while others won't even be considered by the customer unless they're trusted.

Securing the testimonials

How do you get these testimonials? Start with your current customers, of course. As you've noticed, I consistently talk about identifying your "best customer," the type of person who contributes the most to your bottom line. Since that's who you want to attract with these (and just about any other) ads, you need people just like them for the testimonials. You want their neighbors.

Approach your good repeat customers and just ask them if they'll help you. Explain what you're going to do and why they're such an important part of the effort. As you might expect, you should be prepared to be turned down by most of the people you ask. Many folks are shy, don't want to be bothered, or are afraid of looking foolish in the media. There are enough people around, though, who will be excited by the chance to grab fifteen minutes of fame that it's worth the effort.

Some of your prospects will want some form of compensation—but make it clear that you can't give any because it would undermine their credibility. This rule even applies to future discounts you might give them, too. If you have a way of offering preferential treatment to certain customers (no standing in line, free delivery, or free gift wrapping, for example) you might offer it, but even that's no-no if other customers have to pay to get it. A big part of your message's credibility depends on the purity of the testifier's motivation.

Keep recruiting until you have about a dozen potential endorsers. You're going to need more than you think because some of them are going to turn out to be unsuitable or will change their minds about participating.

Producing the ads

Have each one of them sign a permission form that allows you to use their likeness, voice, and appearance for commercial purposes. This is absolutely essential to avoid potential legal problems. You can get standard forms from your ad sales rep, the company producing your ads, or a professional photographer's supply house.

The production itself requires a little time and patience. You want your ad to sound spontaneous, unrehearsed, and genuine. The only way to achieve that effect is to make it happen that way. Let them speak in their natural way, using their own words, and say the things they want to say. If you write out what you want your endorsers to say, they'll never sound sincere.

The procedure is pretty simple although it depends somewhat on the media you'll be using. An interviewer (you or a third party) talks to each endorser and records their conversation (using commercial-quality audio or video media). This can be done individually, in a group, in their home, or even in your store. The conversations are then professionally edited to fit the desired advertising message.

You should have a series of questions you might ask to send them in the direction you want them to go, but let them answer in their own words. Make your questions open-ended to encourage them to talk. "Yes" or "no" answers won't help you at all. Here are a few open-ended questions to get you started:

Why did you buy your last _____ from _____?

What do you like most about _____?

Tell me about the shopping experience at _____.

What would you tell your neighbor about _____?

The answers to questions like these will be natural, sincere, and hopefully very usable in your ads.

The satisfied customer testimonial can be adapted for just about any medium. TV and radio are obvious choices. Don't forget online outlets like YouTube, your blogs, and social media sites. You can also use them in print, though, along with pictures of the endorsers. The same holds true for direct mail and even billboards. Since the format is so adaptable, it works very well in a media mix.

Build good relationships

Here's a key step in the process. Once the ads are produced—but before they appear—show them to the endorsers and make sure they're comfortable with the words coming out of their mouths. The last thing you want is to have to pull an ad because the person in it starts complaining. A real nice touch is to give them some copies of the ads as keepsakes. These can be tear sheets of print ads or video or audio cassettes for broadcast media.

As you probably observed, a great deal of the success of this plan depends on two interpersonal relationships: the one between you and the endorser and the one between the endorser and the prospective customer. Good common sense and a healthy dose of the Golden Rule will make your Satisfied Neighbor Testimonials easy to do and highly effective.

Idea 4
The Hands-On Marathon

Not many promotional ideas build traffic, enhance your position in the community, and generate free publicity all at the same time. The Hands-On Marathon does all that and more.

The promotion is designed to bring crowds to your business location in three ways: with advertising, word of mouth, and free news coverage. Since it involves a group of individuals raising money for a local charitable cause, it also polishes your image as an upstanding member of your community. And it's unique, timely, and photogenic enough to appeal to the news media as well.

The event works something like a charity dance marathon—only just about anybody can take part. Participants solicit pledges of donations based on the amount of time they can keep both their hands in physical contact with a large item in your store window or parking lot. The person who holds on the longest wins a prize. The money raised, of course, goes to a local worthy cause.

Promotion components

There aren't many parts to this promotion and the concept is simple, which makes it easy to run and advertise effectively.

The prize can be just about anything of enough value to motivate participation. Ideally, of course, it's best if it's an item that you sell since you'll get the greatest value from the publicity pictures that way. It also helps if it's large enough to physically accommodate a number of participants, although that's not essential. A few prizes come immediately to mind: A car, a boat, a suite of furniture. But you could also construct a gigantic gift box with a picture of a diamond ring on it, too. Using the gift box approach allows you to ignore size and give away almost anything.

Choose the charity with some care. You may have a favorite cause that you regularly support. Before you choose it, though, be honest with yourself about how popular it is with your customers. The wider the appeal of the charity, the more likely it is to draw contestants and generate free publicity.

There are both plusses and minuses to choosing a national cause. The plus side is that they have wide appeal and an infrastructure to help you. The minus, though, is that most of them already have strong fund-raising events—even telethons and walkathons—that can compete with yours. And scheduling your event as part of theirs is not a good idea, either, because yours can easily get lost in the overall hoopla.

Another factor to consider is how much support the organization can give you. Will they recruit participants? Distribute rules and pledge forms? Provide judges for the contest? Arrange for news coverage? Direct traffic? Any functions they perform are ones that you don't have to, which frees you and your staff to run your business during the promotion. Just make sure they have the ability to do the things you ask, especially publicity. They many (or may not) have contacts in the media, but you'll want to write the press releases and other material—or at least see them before distribution—to make sure your message gets out.

Rules and precautions

There are some practical health and safety concerns with this promotion, so it's a good idea to take simple precautions and set up a few ground rules.

Establish a minimum age for the participants. If you want to include kids, hold a separate, less intense event for them with a time limit. They collect pledges, but their event lasts a maximum of two or three hours and everyone who goes the distance wins a small prize. If the response is great enough, you might even have separate divisions for pre-teens and high schoolers.

Limit the number of adult participants by requiring a minimum amount of pledges to enter (at least $500). They should also sign a consent form that indemnifies you, your business, and the charity organization. This goes for the kids' parents, too. If the charity doesn't have an attorney to write one, invest a few dollars in one yourself. You may also want to have a health care professional on hand for emergencies.

The contest rules are pretty simple:

- Contestants must stand without touching the prize with any part of their body except their hands.

- They must keep both hands in continuous contact with the object. (If they scratch their nose, they're out.)

- They can't receive any physical assistance or support from anyone else including the other contestants.

- There will be one five-minute break every hour. This is the only time they can leave the object, visit the restroom, or receive any refreshments.

- If either hand leaves the object or they break any of the other rules, they are eliminated.

- The judges will eliminate contestants and calculate the time achieved. Their decisions are final.

- The contest will end when the next to last contestant breaks contact or at a specific time (like 8PM of the last day).

If there's a tie, the grand prize will be awarded by random drawing from among those still in contention. The others receive a consolation prize. You can also award prizes for things like the most pledges collected or most outlandish attire. If local law allows, you can increase the excitement and raise extra money for the cause by letting spectators buy chances on the winner.

The marathon runs continuously, of course, so you'll need judges and support people around the clock. You'll also need food and drink for the contestants and sufficient rest room facilities to handle them during their breaks.

Promoting the event

There are four stages in the advertising of the event. First, announce the event and recruit participants. This can use narrowly targeted media, since the pool of prospective participants is rather small. Your copy for this phase should make the contestant feel warm and fuzzy for helping out the charity, capitalize on their desire to win the prize, and appeal to their competitive nature and sense of adventure. The call to action is to have them visit your store for their pledge sheets and entry forms—and to ogle the grand prize.

The second stage supports the participants as they solicit pledges. This has more general audience appeal and the copy should play up the connection to the charity, how much good it does for the community, and how important this event is to the cause. Don't forget to plug your business, too, though, and to give the customer a reason to buy. You can also ask donors to come to your store to make their pledge as another traffic-builder.

The third stage of the advertising is for the event itself. You should use seventy percent of your budget for this portion and schedule it pretty heavy for the two weeks prior to the weekend. Present the Hands-On Marathon as a fun spectator event with lots of suspense and the potential for some good-natured fun. Refreshments and door prizes are always a good touch, too, and urge the spectators to make a donation while they're there.

Devote about half the copy to selling your merchandise, since now's the time to reap some profit from the promotion. If it makes economic sense, put some sale pricing in effect, keep the store open 24 hours, or bring in some promotional merchandise.

The fourth stage comes the week after the promotion. Run some ads thanking the community for its support, congratulating the winner, and touting the amount of money you raised for the charity. You might want to schedule an "appreciation sale" for that week as well.

News coverage

All of these advertising stages should correspond to some intense public relations activity. If you don't already have one, compile a list of local news media. It should include the names of the news directors or editors-in-chief along with their fax numbers, email addresses, and other general contact information. Your charity partner can probably help with this. They may also have some news outlets of their own, such as contributor/member newsletters or web sites.

Send a one-page press release to this list at every stage of the promotion. That includes when you announce it, when you choose the charity that will benefit, when you select a prize, when you open it for entries, when the judges are named, and so on. Frequency is more important than anything else, so don't put all your news in one release. When you contact the news media you should play up the charity support angle rather than the merchandising aspects of the promotion, of course. Don't hesitate to speak to reporters personally, and make it clear you are available for interviews at any time.

The weekend of the event, call the names on your list and personally invite them for a photo session. You'll probably get pretty good response since most media are starved for hard news on weekends. Take plenty of pictures of your own, too, and distribute them with your press releases announcing the winners, awarding the check to the charity (two separate ones!), and so on.

The Hands-On Marathon can be a lot of fun for your customers and staff. It will put your business in the community spotlight, generate traffic, and help a worthy cause. It's a combination that's hard to beat.

Idea 5

How To Buy Anything

Shopping for a home computer can be like trying to buy a new car from someone who only speaks Mongolian. You both know what the thing looks like and does, but getting enough information to make an informed purchase decision is next to impossible.

A situation like this frustrates the consumer. For the retailer, though, it's an opportunity to create a strong point of difference from the competition. You can stake out a position in the market that will increase your shopper-to-buyer conversion ratio, build customer loyalty, and generate fabulous word-of-mouth.

The idea is to teach your prospect how to buy your product.

Most advertising tells the prospect what to buy and gives them reasons to buy it. That's fine for small-ticket items with few complex features. The customer sees the benefit and can make their purchase decision with little doubt that they're making a mistake. Even if they do buy the "wrong" item, their investment in money and decision-making time is so small it's no big deal if it's lost.

But big-ticket items are different. Cars, mutual funds and other investments, appliances and the like are complex items with many options to choose from and many features that differentiate one brand from another. They're not usually bought on impulse so the customer may invest days or even weeks of shopping time before making a decision. The purchase involves a significant amount of money, too, so a "wrong" decision can be painful.

A big source of customer frustration is wading through unfamiliar terms, mind-numbing specifications, and confusing feature comparisons. The merchant who takes some of the pain out of the process stands a good chance of winning the customer. The way to do that is to teach, not to tell.

Become a teacher

Start by choosing the most important decision factors in purchasing your product. These aren't necessarily the features that differentiate your product from the competitions', but rather the ones that the prospect should know about and understand to make an informed decision. If you sell computers they might be memory, software, and ease of setup. For re-frigerators these features might be capacity, energy efficiency, and options like ice dispensers. These factors are probably the ones the customers ask about most often, so they're not hard to choose.

Now write a very short non-technical description of each feature. Each description will be in a separate message, so make them self-contained. A good place to start is often with a definition of a term associated with the item. Then explain how it's measured or quantified. Finally, tie the explanation to a benefit so the customer knows why this information is important to them.

Brevity is important. People learn best when they're dealing with small bits of information about a single subject. That's why you only want one feature in each message. Attention spans are short and getting shorter, so streamline your message to get as much of it in as possible before the audience's attention wanders.

Simplicity counts, too. You don't want to teach the customer how to build a refrigerator, just how to read energy efficiency ratings so they can make apples-to-apples comparisons. You're not trying to show off how much you know, either. You're trying to show the customer how easy you can make their buying process.

A good test of your message is to ask a "layperson" to critique it. Find someone who isn't an expert in what you sell and see if they think your information is clear and helpful.

As strange as it sounds, resist the temptation to slant the information you're giving to favor your products. One of the reasons this approach works so well is that the consumer comes to see you as an objective advisor to them rather than as a shill promoting in your own merchandise. The credibility you establish rubs off on your other advertising messages and your sales staff, so you don't want to endanger it by hinting at bias.

A media bonus

Here's another reason to make your message informative rather than persuasive: free media!

It's very possible that your consumer-friendly message can be positioned as valuable information the media can treat as editorial content. TV and radio stations can use it as a feature in their news or talk shows. It can make good filler for the lifestyle section of the newspaper. And blogs (including yours!) are generally crying for no-cost content so your message could easily find a place online. It's not hard to turn your copy into a 500-1,000-word article that can be syndicated through online content providers like articlecity.com or goarticles.com.

You'll need to present the media with a complete package so that their staff won't have to do anything—and so you'll have as much editorial control as possible. Tell them you'll write and produce the messages yourself, handing them a finished recording or layout to use.

Promise enough different messages to make them regular features. To establish a weekly feature, for example, you'll need 13 different messages.

The medium can run one per week with four repeats in a year without alienating the audience. Give them all 13 finished messages at once, too. It'll be easier for them and for you.

By the way, don't overlook your local PBS radio and TV stations. These aren't commercial messages, so they can run them without violating their charter. A small underwriting pledge or donation from you won't hurt anything, though.

You might find a commercial medium that will accept your proposal with no strings attached. It's much more likely, however, that some money will need to change hands. The truly complete package will not only have the messages but a sponsor for them as well—you, of course.

Offer to pay for an ad or airtime equal to that given to the informative message. In other words, if your feature is a 30-second vignette, offer to buy a 30-second spot to run along with it. And, since you'll be sponsoring the feature, ask for a billboard to go along with it. (A billboard is the sponsor identification: "This informed consumer message is brought to you by...")

Tying it all together

The commercial or ad in your sponsored feature should match your regular selling message. In fact, it's advisable to use the same copy for both. When you do, the consumer who sees your informative message will be reminded of it when they see your commercial message, giving the latter more credibility and memorability.

Your "How To Buy" message can be used in other ways, too. Put some signs defining terms used (RAM, BTU, kHz) around your store. Turn your messages into bullet points that can go on store signage as well. Include them in any direct mail pieces, newsletters, or pre-prints you distribute. You might want to print some brochures containing all your messages for distribution at the cash register or elsewhere.

Finally, don't forget your staff. For this campaign to be truly effective, the consumer has to sense the same helpful, informative attitude when they come in the store as they do in the messages. A few brief training sessions will help establish this mindset and improve the customer experience.

Idea 6

Frozen Ropes

Once upon a time there was a car company. They wanted to build traffic for their dealers, create warm feelings in their customers, and enhance their brand's action-orientated image. So they invited (traffic) kids (warm feelings) to their dealers to play football (action).

I'm referring to the NFL's Punt Pass and Kick Contest, which was a highly successful promotion for Ford Motor Company and its dealers for years. It's still around, too with a variety of sponsors. Frozen Ropes is a variation on the theme build around baseball instead of football—and with adults as well as kids as participants. After all, very few Little Leaguers buy cars, lawn mowers, or motorcycles.

Almost any sport can be used, of course, with the simple guideline that the more popular the sport, the more successful the promotion will be. Soccer and basketball would be winners. Badminton and hurling probably wouldn't be.

The contest

The concept is simple. "Frozen Ropes," for those who aren't fans, is a baseball term for a line drive, or a ball hit so hard that it travels in a straight line instead of an arc. During May when youth baseball is at its peak, you sponsor a weekend contest in your parking lot or other space near your store. Entrants vie to see who can hit a softball the farthest.

The rules are pretty simple, too. The ball is hit off a practice "tee" instead of being pitched to the batter. That levels the playing field and actually reduces the distance the ball will fly. You use a softball instead of a hardball because it won't travel nearly as far. The batter gets three swings and the ball has to come to rest within the boundaries of an area no more than thirty yards wide. A small flag is stuck in the ground where the longest ball stops moving so that subsequent contestants can see how far they have to hit to win.

The gorilla who wins receives a grand prize related to your business (like a lease on an SUV for a year). Runner-up and consolation prizes can be awarded, too.

The community connection

Anyone can enter on the day of the contest, but there are a couple of prerequisites to make the promotion more appealing and (profitable).

First, they have to pay to play. Each entrant pays a nominal entry fee (like $10) which is donated to the youth baseball league in your area. This feature is a great PR move and can generate a lot of support on its own.

The league will probably be happy to help you publicize the event with announcements and signs at games and in any newsletters or other mailings they do. You should also ask for a list of team sponsors so you can approach them to post a sign in their business or other help in promoting the cause.

The sales connection

The other prerequisite is less altruistic. You can require the entrants to supply their full names, contact info, and even some demographic/income or purchase intention information right on the entry form. Just keep the number of questions under five to increase response.

You can use that information in several ways. Add the entrants to your prospect database or mailing list (or start one if you don't have one now).

Send each of them a postcard the week after the event with a coupon to thank them for participating. The info will also provide leads for your sales staff.

Traffic

One of the goals of this promotion is to bring traffic to your location, but traffic isn't an end in itself. You need to take advantage of it while you have it. Almost no one will come to enter the contest alone; they'll bring families and friends. Rope off the contest and spectator area so that the entrants have to go through your store or showroom to get there. Set up the registration table inside the store so that the spectators will mill around while their champion is filling out his or her form.

Fill the place with signage about your products and services, have plenty of product literature spread around, and place salespeople at strategic locations to answer questions. Instruct the sales staff to refrain from the hard sell, though, so that the spectators have a positive experience that will encourage them to come back.

You can also have a simple no-entry-fee drawing which the spectators enter in the store by filling out a simple name and contact information form. You'll use the information collected as outlined above. This also gives the spectators another reason to stay in the store for a few minutes.

Precautions and rules

This promotion is so straightforward that there aren't too many pit-falls. Entrants should sign an indemnification release, of course, in the wild event that they hurt themselves (or someone else) swinging the bat. The hitting and landing area should be kept spectator-free and a portable batting cage to stop pop-ups might not be a bad idea.

You should provide all the equipment—for the sake of fairness as well as safety. Give the entrants a few bats of different weights to choose from, but don't let them use their own.

You'll need judges to mark and measure the distances. Their decisions will be final, of course, and no entrants or spectators can be allowed to enter the "field" both to prevent tampering and for safety. I strongly suggest that the distance be measured from the batting tee to the spot where the ball comes to rest rather than where it lands. The touch-down area can be rather subjective but there can be no arguments about where the ball stops rolling.

It's not a bad idea to have separate contests for men, women, and kids. These can go on concurrently, with different flags used to mark each category's leader.

Promoting the event

In addition to enlisting the support of the local sports leagues, you'll need to do some paid media promotion as well in order to fully capitalize on the idea.

Start the promotion about three weeks before the weekend of the event. Ramp up the exposure as you go and really hit it hard the three days immediately preceding.

Almost any local media can be used. Ones with some sports content should be your first choice. This can mean TV news, sports highlight shows, and live sports coverage. You might also consider cable TV sports channels. Your newspaper's sports section works, too. A sports radio station (or even just a radio sports talk show) is a natural choice and if you can persuade some sports radio personalities to compete, you'll strike promotional golf.

Another place to look for exposure is in local sports facilities. Minor league ballparks, commercial driving ranges and batting cages, even the local "Y" might be willing to put up a poster to support youth baseball.

Finally, make the media a big part of your promotion during the planning stages. Tell your ad sales reps what you've got in mind and see what they can come up with to sweeten their packages. They might be willing to not only publicize the event, but to provide prizes, entry forms, signage, and even some on-air sports talent to MC the contest. They'll probably want co-sponsorship billing, but that's OK. You want the traffic—not the glory—don't you?

Idea 7
Safe Kids

Not every business needs or even wants traffic. Buying cycles and purchase patterns can dictate a less "buy it now" and more "keep us in mind" approach. A bank, insurance agency, or public utility, for example, generally wants to do "image" advertising rather than traffic-building promotions.

"Image" or "positioning" advertising is fine, but it tends to get lost in the clutter and noise of all other types of commercial messages. To make your image campaign stand out, attach it to a sponsorship of something like the Safe Kids campaign.

There are two parts to this campaign, not including your commercial message. The first is the safety message itself and the second is the contest you run to encourage kids to learn the material you present.

The safety message

In general, each month you sponsor a message about a different safety topic that applies to kids' safety. These messages will be similar to the public service announcements and ads you see on the local media. The difference is that your sponsorship of this message takes it out of the realm of the unpaid (and therefore seldom aired) and into the category of paid sponsorships, which are not only aired in better positions but stand out from the clutter of ads around them.

There are dozens of topics, but here are six to get you started:

- Bicycle and skate safety
- Latch-key living

- Swimming safety

- Traffic hazards

- Household poisons

- Dealing with strangers

You can turn to your local police, fire, and public health departments for content. Other sources of information include the automobile association, Red Cross, and various federal agencies. Many of these organizations will have prepared messages you can use verbatim (with their permission, of course). If not, they may be willing to assign a staff member to write a message for the medium you're using.

The safe kids contest

To increase your audience's involvement with your message, hold a simple contest that requires the kids to pay attention to it. The entry form is a questionnaire with three questions about that month's safety topic. Forms with all three questions answered correctly are placed in a drawing for a prize like a bike helmet or even a savings bond.

You can distribute the forms in your locations. But since traffic isn't something your business needs or wants, you can also distribute them elsewhere. Other potential distribution points include the organizations you enlisted to help prepare the campaign, schools, libraries, and churches, and even non-competing commercial establishments that cater to the family trade. A fast food restaurant or supermarket chain, for example, might very well be interested in distributing the entry forms in return for mentions in your promotional messages.

Using the media

The Safe Kids campaign can be adapted to just about any commercial medium. For radio, broadcast TV or cable TV, the format includes an opening sponsor ID, your commercial message, then the safety message. The last couple of lines in the safety message encourage contest entries and promote the entry form pickup locations.

Newspapers, shoppers, and other print media can be used also. Just lay out your ad to encompass the safety message in a box or window within the commercial ad space.

When choosing your media, keep in mind the desired demographics of your target audience. That audience should primarily consist of families with young children (under 12), which generally means adults in the 25-40 age group. You might also have a secondary demographic target based on the income, education, or employment of your best prospective customer.

As odd as it may seem, I suggest you stay away from programs or editorial content that's intended purely for kids. One reason for this strategy is that you want to reach the parents (not the kids alone) because the adults are your ultimate prospects. Another is that there is a great deal of sensitivity about advertising directed at kids, and you don't want to be perceived as an ogre preying on their impressionable young minds. Finally, the parents are the ones who are going to encourage the kids to pay attention to the messages so they can enter the contest.

You should be able to negotiate a favorable deal with the local media. Expect to pay standard rates for your commercial message, but ask for the safety message to be delivered gratis. At the very least you should expect to pay for the time or space it occupies at a heavily discounted rate.

There is also a possibility that the organizations providing the safety message content may have funds available to defray some of the costs. This can be in the form of partial payment for your media or for covering the cost of producing the safety message. They also may be able and willing to help in the prize department. Even if they can't supply the grand prize, they might have small items to distribute to all the entrants who answer all three questions correctly. These can include such items as T-shirts, stickers, and books.

The Safe Kids campaign will increase the impact of your commercial messages, establish your business as one concerned about your customers' well-being, and give your prospects a reason to remember you.

Idea 8

The Weekend Media Extravaganza

Do you need a really quick traffic-building boost?

Sometimes you're facing a flat quarter and need a quick burst of sales to beat last year. Or you need to put some sparkle on your image. Or your staff is on autopilot and needs a jolt to wake them up. A short promotion with some star appeal will fit the bill. That's the Weekend Media Extravaganza.

It's built around a personal appearance by a local media celebrity. You may not be able to book Oprah Winfrey or Taylor Swift to sign autographs in your store, but you can probably arrange for a local radio, TV, or even newspaper personality to be there. And they may not cost as much as you think.

Don't underestimate their drawing power, either. The guy or gal that does the sports on your local TV station has a sort of aura that comes from being on screen. The morning radio personality can pull in a certain audience with wit, charm, or outrageous behavior. Even the local newspaper hunting and fishing columnist has a personal following. They wouldn't be in those positions if they couldn't draw an audience. And a surprisingly large segment of that audience will make an effort to see them in person.

Enlarging the appeal

A personal appearance by itself, however, will only appeal to that market segment that feels it's worth their while just to get to see the personality. You can enhance the celebrity's drawing power by giving the public some chance to interact with them. If you can remove the invisible wall between the stage and the seats, so to speak, that will help. And if you can somehow tie the personality's interaction to your merchandise or services, so much the better.

For example, a restaurant could have the personality join each table for a few minutes of conversation with the customers. At an appliance store the personality could take part in a cooking demonstration with small groups of customers. If you sell cars, the customer might be offered the opportunity to take a test drive along with the personality. The idea is to put the personality and the customer into a one-to-one (or one-to-few) situation involving your merchandise.

You'll want to make the appearance a real event (this is an Extravaganza, remember?), so add some bells and whistles. Free stuff is always good. Merchandise samples, coupons, and other store-related items are an obvious choice. Don't overlook food, either. Hot dogs, soft drinks, balloons, popcorn—full tummies make happier customers.

You can probably also negotiate some goodies from the media, too. Pictures of the personality for autographing are an obvious choice. But most radio and TV stations also have T-shirts, caps, bumper stickers, refrigerator magnets and the like imprinted with their logo. You might want to ask the station to provide some giveaways with your logo, too. If you have to, it might well be worthwhile to foot part of the bill for these items.

Signing the celebrity

So how do you make all this happen? Don't call the personality and ask them—they'll either turn you down flat or ask for an appearance fee. Ask your ad sales rep from that station or publication instead. You're going to advertise the event anyway so tell them what you have in mind and see what kind of package they can come up with. They may well be able to include the appearance at no charge or at a much-reduced fee since many talent contracts have provisions for personal appearances by station personnel.

On the other hand, it's also very common for many stations to restrict or prohibit certain personalities from appearing at these types of events. Reporters and news anchors are almost always off limits. The meteorologist and sports anchor may or may not be. Talk show hosts and DJ's, though, are almost always available. In fact, since these appearances help promote the station's programming, they are usually eager to make them.

When you talk to the rep, make your request fairly open-ended. The ad sales rep may have some features he or she can throw into the deal that you're not aware of. Sponsorship of special programming that airs around the date and time of your event may be available. The newspaper may be planning a circulation sweepstakes with prizes that can be displayed in your store. You'll find out about these things if you encourage the rep to be creative.

There are some other elements that can contribute to the promotion's success. Many radio stations have standard remote broadcast packages that include all the things we've mentioned and more. Just make sure that the deal includes a well-known personality from the station, not just an engineer with some equipment. It's the personality that's going to draw the crowd, not the remote broadcast. See "Broadcasting Live" for some other ideas on remote broadcasts.

Make your ads work

The copy strategy is pretty simple. Personality, date, location. Those are the three points to drive home. If you can weave in some positioning statements that's all for the better, but make sure that these three key points are repeated several times. That means three times in a thirty-second spot, five times in a sixty, and as both the headline and the tag line in print.

Naturally, the media outlet for this promotion is going to be largely determined by the personality you choose. In fact, some of the other media may not allow you to advertise the appearance because it will promote one of their competitors. It doesn't hurt to ask, of course, but don't be surprised. Don't overlook online opportunities, either. Use your social media network, blogs, etc., but also encourage the personality to promote the appearance on their Facebook page, Tweets, and other places.

Don't scrimp on media

This is a one-time event, not an ongoing campaign, so schedule your media accordingly. Start the promotion three weeks ahead of your event date. You want to create excitement and it's difficult to maintain a high level of audience enthusiasm much longer than that. Their decision to attend will also be more spur of the moment than planned, so exposure too far in advance will be wasted. Don't make it too last minute, though, because you need exposure over time to drive the message home. Three weeks is about right.

Buy more exposure than you think you need. There are no second chances to make this promotion work, so now is not the time to cut corners with the media schedule. You only have three weeks, too, so don't spend any of that time "ramping up" your exposure. You may want to double up Thursday and Friday before the event, but that's about it. In other words, you're media spending should go from heavy to very heavy.

The frequency of your messages is more important than their reach, too, which also means you need a heavy schedule. Sprinkle a few drive-time radio spots in, but really saturate the other dayparts. The same with TV. Use a little prime time if it's not too expensive, but put ninety percent of your budget into cheaper times when you can get more spots for your money. In the newspaper, place several smaller ads in each edition rather than one big one. Most of your advertising will be on one medium, so you'll have some leverage in the negotiations.

One other point about buying media for this (or any other one-time promotion): If you're going to buy just one newspaper ad each week or three TV spots, don't even bother. You need BIG exposure to have a BIG event. This is not a weekend nap. It's a Weekend Extravaganza!

Idea 9

Real People

Service industries represent the largest segment of our economy. To most people, "service" means attention to their needs by a company's staff.

Increasingly, though, you don't encounter informed, helpful staff members at many businesses. Their phone is answered by an automated operator and your message is taken by voice mail. You place your order by entering it on a keypad and pay for it by swiping your credit card. The ATM handles your banking, the self-service pump dispenses your gas (while you wash your own windshield), and you buy your books online.

Technology may improve productivity, but very few customers establish long-term relationships with a computer. To attract and keep your customers with something other than price promotions, you need people. As the name implies, that's what this campaign is all about.

Sell your staff

If you offer personal service to your customers, it's a great idea to promote it as a way to distinguish your business from your competitors. But you can't just say you provide personal service, you have to demonstrate it. Today's consumer is so jaded by advertising promises that they only believe what they see.

So sell your staff along with your services. In the Real People campaign, you feature a different staff member in your ad each month. You show them providing one of the services you sell. The campaign doesn't just make a claim, it proves the claim to be true.

The Real People campaign also has a side benefit: it helps build employee morale. By choosing one of your employees to represent your business to the public, you're sending them a very clear message that they're important to you—that you depend on them for your success. It's one thing to put that thought into a mission statement and quite another to put it into practice.

Raising morale raises profits, too. Motivated employees treat your customers better, which increases sales and encourages repeat business. Employees who feel valued are less likely to leave for another job and reducing staff turnover reduces your recruiting and training expenses.

Executing the concept

How many different services do you provide? If you make an inventory of them, you might be surprised at how many different ways you serve your customers. There are the obvious ones, of course, like taking orders and delivery. But do your employees (and you) do any other tasks like assembling merchandise, gift-wrapping, shipping, installing, etc.? Whether you charge for these services or include them in the price of your goods, each one can be featured in an ad.

You'll be tempted to make an overall glowing claim about your many services then list them all as proof of your claim. But a list is hard for the consumer to remember and it prevents you from showing the service being performed, so choose one service at a time to promote in your campaign. Plan on using a different service each month, even if you have to repeat them.

Preferably, an employee who actually provides that service will be featured in your ad—and identified by name. Once again, it's important to use only one person in each ad. The only way the consumer is going to believe that these are "real people" is by getting to know them. That means the employee has to be on screen for most of the commercial time or occupy a large portion of the ad space.

Choosing the Real People

If you have a very small staff, the job of choosing an employee to feature each month is easy. During the course of the year, you'll probably be able to use everybody at least once.

If you have more than 12 employees, though, you obviously have to leave some out—at least during the first year. There are several ways to select the soon-to-be famous employees. One is to make a subjective choice yourself based on criteria like how well they perform the services they provide. This method allows you to reward your super stars with something other than money. The downside is that the others may feel slighted or grouse that you play favorites.

Another option is to hold a competition based on some objective measurements like sales made or number of packages processed. This removes the favoritism problem but raises the possibility that those who know they are too far behind to win will just stop trying, with the result that the overall quality of your service actually declines.

The procedure I particularly like is to have the staff choose the featured employee by secret ballot. You establish some simple rules (like no one can be featured two months in a row) and maybe even do the nominating (to ensure "quality control"), but the employees make the actual choice.

Whatever method you use, don't try to choose only the most photogenic employee or the one that speaks most effectively. The goal of the campaign is to convince the customer that, when they do business with you, they will experience the same kind of great service they're seeing in your advertising. If they think the employee in the ad is a professional model or performer, that belief will be impaired.

Remember, "real people" have blemishes, cowlicks, and love handles, so don't be afraid to let those features be seen in your ads. And, while it's not essential, it may be best to not give the featured employee a non-speaking role in the ad. This helps you avoid stage fright and other production problems.

Media strategy

Real People can run in just about any medium or media mix. It's particularly suited for visual exposure, though, and putting it on television (either broadcast or cable) allows you to truly demonstrate the service your selling.

This is not a short-term quick-fix promotion. It's a campaign that needs exposure over time to establish your position as the premier service provider in your market. So give it time to grow and plan on running it continually over a year or more. You can produce many of the ads at one time to economize production, but only run one each month. The repetition keeps your message clear and improves retention. Changing monthly is more than sufficient to keep the message fresh.

Legalities and contingencies

There's really only one precaution you should take: have the featured employee sign a commercial release allowing you to use their likeness in your ads. Whether you compensate them for their appearance or not, you should have this layer of protection just in case.

What happens if the featured employee leaves for greener pastures? The release they sign should be written to cover your rights to use their likeness whether they are an employee or not, so you are protected on that front. And, since you're only going to run the ad for a month, there's very little threat to your credibility.

There are a couple of nice touches you can add to the campaign. Take a still picture from each month's ad and have it blown up into a poster to hang in your store. When the month is over, give that poster to the featured employee as a keepsake. Displaying the poster reminds the entire staff that you're selling the quality of their service and giving it to the employee is a small thanks for their help.

Idea 10
Life Stages

What does a young newlywed couple have in common with a pair of late-middle-aged empty nesters? Very little—at least in terms of finances and consumption. Consumers aren't a homogenous mass with identical needs, dreams, likes or dislikes. That's why a good marketer will define segments of the total market and address each one differently. Several elements in your marketing strategy, including the type of merchandise offered, the tone of the message, and the media chosen, should be different for individual market segments.

There are many ways to define market segments, including by stages of life. Depending on what products or services you sell, there are almost always distinct differences between the needs of your customers at one point in their life and at another. A furniture store, for example, might have one message aimed at the young newlyweds who need to furnish their first apartment and another for those empty nesters who are ready (and financially able) to upgrade their décor now that the children are out of the house.

The first step in implementing the Life Stages strategy is to define the different points on your customer's timeline. These stages are usually—but certainly not always—age-related. Once you have defined your market life stage segments, distill the needs and prime buying motivator for each segment. Following are a few examples of life stages beginning with the post-education period. This list is by no means definitive but yours can be if you know your customers well.

Life Stage	Description	Needs	Purchase Factors
First Job Holder	Fresh out of school and entering the workforce full time.	Inexpensive transportation, workplace clothes, quick and convenient meals.	Style, fashion
Young Newlyweds	Establishing a household and planning for the future.	Inexpensive furnishings and household goods, savings for the first home.	Selection, price
Early Parents	The first child is in the house, careers are building, and life is becoming complicated.	Expanded living space, more furnishings, new kinds of entertainment, different financial products.	Ease of use, value, safety, durability
Late Parents	Established family, peak earning years.	College savings, more cars for more drivers, recreation and vacations.	Status, quality
Empty Nesters	No children at home, retirement approaching, more disposable income.	Scaled back living expenses but expanded discretionary spending, retirement plans.	Luxury, fulfillment
Early Retirees	Leaving the job market, adjusting to different incomes, lifestyle and pace.	Greater health-care needs, more manageable living space, more recreation.	Ease of acquisition, safety, enjoyment

Now examine your inventory of merchandise and services to match the items that have the greatest appeal to each market segment. These will be the featured items in your Life Stages campaign.

Unifying the Life Stages campaign

Most businesses don't cater to just one life stage market segment. A bank will have services for many different kinds of customers just like a department store has departments for people with particular interests. One of the keys to the success of the Life Stages campaign is to create a message that will appeal to the target segment while not excluding the others. The furniture store doesn't want the empty nesters to think that they only offer inexpensive apartment-scale merchandise if they are exposed to the ads aimed at the newlyweds.

That's where a good slogan, jingle, logo or other mnemonic (memory aiding) device comes in. In this campaign it's used consistently in all the ads to remind each market segment that there's something in the store for them, too. Ideally, it will also contain a reference to the prime benefit customers experience when they do business with you.

The best unifying device will be applicable in all of your advertising media. You may believe, for example that you only need a visual logo since you only plan to advertise in the newspaper. But it's a good idea to consider an audio version as well because of the media considerations discussed below. Your unifying device should be adaptable and immediately recognizable whether its exposed aurally, visually, or both.

Media considerations

As with most of these marketing ideas, Life Stages can be successfully executed in several different media. In fact, you should plan to use different media to reach individual market segments because of their divergent media habits and preferences. Conventional wisdom, for example, says that young people are heavy online users while older ones are more dependable newspaper readers. A little research (and common sense) will help you be even more specific about your media choices.

Radio stations target fairly narrow age demographics that allow efficient segment reach. Television, both broadcast and cable, offers individual programs with widely different appeals to individual segments. The same is true for magazines and web sites, blogs, and social media networks. The ultimate targeting medium, of course, is direct mail, which allows you to reach market segments with pinpoint accuracy.

Reach is not the only consideration when choosing media, however. Nor is cost. One of the most important factors you should take into account is each medium's ability to convey the message and evoke the response you need from the consumer. Life Stages is designed in many applications to evoke an emotional response that will guide future purchases rather than a more visceral reaction prompting a buying action today. This is particularly true for businesses like banks, stockbrokers, insurance agencies, and hospitals, where the buying decision is not necessarily a purely rational, fact-driven one.

When you are trying to achieve an emotional response, visual media are hard to beat—and video tops the list of alternatives. Video lets you wrap your selling message in little "mini-dramas" that reflect the viewer-customer's own life. It can very effectively position your product or service as the solution to the characters'—and therefore your customers—problems. You can achieve some of these effects with other media, but not nearly as well as with video, whether online, cable, or broadcast.

Life Stages execution

Life Stages is a long-term campaign designed to last (and work for) years so it requires some planning and forethought. It's flexible in terms of the specific merchandise or sales events promoted, but needs to be rigid when it comes to the use of your unifying device.

Each message should contain these four elements:

- An attention-getting device
- A targeted merchandise or service offer
- A market segment-specific benefit (reason to buy)
- A unifying mnemonic device.

The attention-getting device may be market segment-specific, but it doesn't have to be. It should be changed frequently, though, because even the strongest attention-getter loses impact with overexposure. The merchandise or service offered to each segment can be changed for seasonality or other reasons, but the unifying device should remain constant.

Idea 11

Brought To You By

Your customers are assailed by commercial messages. They see thirty or more spots and promotional announcements every hour they watch television or listen to the radio. The content of their daily newspaper is more than two-thirds advertising. The streets they drive are lined with billboards and signs. Estimates vary, but your customers are exposed to as many as 3,000 commercial messages every day.

How do you get them to notice yours?

One way is to wrap your message in content that has special appeal to your customers and a great way to do this is to become a sponsor of an editorial feature. Sponsorships have several distinct advantages over standard ROP (run of press) or ROS (run of schedule) ads.

- A sponsorship gives you an extra link to your customer in the form of identification with the feature or program sponsored.

- It leaves the customer with the feeling that you have given them something of value in addition to the information contained in your commercial message.

- Sponsorships enhance the credibility of your commercial message, since the sponsored feature is objective editorial material, not self-serving advertising.

- It draws extra attention to your commercial message and gives additional name exposure in the form of the billboard or sponsor ID.

- In some sponsorships, the format separates your commercial message from all others, giving it a great opportunity to stand out.

- Your customers pay greater attention to commercial messages connected to features, since they are watching them to get information of interest.

Features to sponsor

The broadcast media are generally more open to sponsorship sales than their competitors in print, although that is changing. Both usually prohibit sponsorship of hard news content in order to preserve their standards of journalistic objectivity. Just about everything else, though, can be sponsored.

The process of choosing a sponsorship begins with considering your best customer. Based on your research of their lifestyles, education, family structure, and so on, what kind of editorial material interests them? One of the principal advantages of sponsorship—the extra attention your commercial message receives—is achievable only when the feature has strong appeal to the customer.

The feature that draws the customer's interest may not relate to your line of merchandise or services, but that's okay. A luxury car dealer, for example, would probably do well to sponsor a report on the stock market or a how-to feature on buying antiques. The dealer's customers will be interested in that information and the commercial message will carry greater impact.

You do, however, have to be careful about how the editorial environment reflects on your business. A positive impact would come, for example, from a fishing report on a boat dealer's message. The same commercial might be viewed negatively, however, if the sponsored feature is about boating accidents. You usually won't be able to dictate the content, so choose your sponsorship opportunity with care.

Broadcast stations (particularly TV) carry two types of programming: national (network or syndicated) and local. Your sponsorship opportunities in national programs are limited by several factors including the amount of commercial time the station can sell. The locally-produced programs, though, are much more flexible—and are of greater interests to the viewer anyway!

What sponsors receive

Each feature on every station will have a different format, but generally a sponsorship will entitle you to a billboard or ID telling the audience that you are bringing them this program, a place within or immediately adjacent to the editorial content for your commercial message, and (sometimes) a closing credit or ID.

In addition to these items, though, there are several others to ask for in your negotiation. Exclusivity is a big one. An exclusive sponsor doesn't share the commercial time in the feature with any other advertiser. That means your commercial message will not be just one more in a long series of spots inflicted on the viewer so it will stand a better chance of being noticed.

You can also ask for an expanded billboard, which contains a selling message in addition to your business name. A standard billboard would say:

"And now here's tonight's weather report, brought to you by DD's Home Improvements."

An expanded billboard might say:

"Tonight's weather report is brought to you by DD's Home Improvements, offering Top Line Awnings to make your deck or patio a more comfortable place to be."

Another key item to request is promotional support. This can take many forms, but the most common are viewership promos for your feature just like those the station airs for its entertainment programs. Here's a simple promo:

"Will you need an umbrella tomorrow? Find out tonight at six during the weather report brought to you by DD's Home Improvements."

Other forms of promotional support are signage for your store, space on the station web site, or imprinting your logo on handouts and giveaways connected to the feature. These items are limited only by your imagination and negotiating ability, so don't be shy about asking.

Finally, the preferred place for your commercial message is during the first third of the feature. This allows the viewer to get interested in the editorial content and then stay tuned during your message in order to hear the rest of the feature. This also more closely identifies your message with the editorial content, which enhances its impact. If your commercial message can't run within the program itself, specify that it be placed after the sponsor ID but before the feature content. The least favorable position is after the feature, when the viewer's attention is more likely to wander.

Sample sponsorship opportunities

There are a remarkable number of sponsorship opportunities on most local radio and TV stations. You'll find plenty of your own simply by viewing or listening to your local stations for that purpose. Here's the list of possibilities from just one small-market television station.

Weather Reports	School Lunch Menus
News Headlines	Business News
Community Interview	Stock Market Report
Newswrap National	Medical Checkup
Sports Reports	Health News
Hot Bowlers Report	Today in History
Weekend Sports in Review	Cooking for Nutrition
Game & Fish Report	Entertainment Reports
Farm Market Prices	About the House – Repairs
Community Calendar	Little Orphan Animal

Finally, keep in mind that sponsorships aren't effective as one-time events. To receive their full marketing value, you need to have consistent exposure over time. This strengthens your association in the customer's mind with the sponsored feature.

A Dozen Holiday Promotions

When you run a business, the holidays are about more than family traditions and general celebrations. For many companies, the volume of sales in the last weeks of the calendar make or break their profits for the year. For others, holiday sales are a welcome bonus to their normal seasonal business pattern. In either case, effective promotions can make your holidays extra merry. Here are an even dozen to round out your year.

Win a refund

Your customers will be dreaming of a white Christmas when they register to win a refund on their gift purchases from your store. One way to do it is to advertise that if it snows on Christmas, the store will draw a lucky winner(s) who will receive a store credit or even a (gasp) cash refund for the purchases they made when they registered. To avoid the hassle of dealing with receipts, the store salesperson or clerk who handles the sale enters the amount of the purchase and initials it on the entry form. A dollar limit can be set, it can apply only to gift certificates, or other simple limitations can be used to control the cost. You also get a big side benefit—a mailing list of the customers who made gift purchases to use for future promotions like Father's Day.

Gift card video

Some people see gift cards or certificates as the ultimate in thoughtlessness. Add a little pizzazz to yours by letting the buyer star in a personalized video greeting to be wrapped with the gift certificate. Set up a laptop with a web camera aimed at a chair in front of a seasonal backdrop of some sort and let the gift-giver record a personal message. To expedite the process, take a tip from TV and provide an "idiot card" (made with a black marker and poster board) containing a standard message they can read aloud. Burn the message to CD and affix a label or slip it into a sleeve with your logo on it, and you've made the customer a walking testimonial for your store. You can conceivably sell these, but considering the cost of blank CDs, you may choose to give them away with the gift certificate purchase.

Wish list

Brides-to-be shouldn't be the only people with a gift registry. Offer your customers a way to register their wish list at your store. You can use a database program or even just a simple paper form that the gift-getter fills out and you file alphabetically for the use of all the friends and relatives they'll send in. You get a bonus, too: a list of items your customer wants but didn't get for Christmas! You could boost January sales with a simple postcard or email to each one that says you're extending the gift-giving season by giving them a discount on the (fill in the blank) that Santa didn't bring.

Santa pet photo

Do you know a professional photographer? Even if you don't, find one and offer them this money-maker. For the price of their donation to the local Humane Society, your customer can bring in their pet and get a professional picture of it with Santa Claus. The photographer sets up in your store on a couple of high-traffic dates and brings along a laptop and ink-dye printer so the pictures can be produced on the spot. He or she will get orders for reprints and Christmas cards plus a new client database.

You'll not only get additional store traffic, but the Humane Society will probably be more than happy to help you publicize the event. Not bad for a no-cost promotion.

Call home

Calling home during the holidays is as traditional as decorating the Christmas tree. A great self-liquidating premium you can make available are prepaid phone cards. You can buy them in bulk at a discount from face value, then pass along the discount to your customers who make a gift purchase during the holidays. Some vendors even offer custom-printed cards and/or a voice message from you every time the card is used.

Donations central

Serving as a collection point for "Toys for Tots" or the local food bank is a good way to generate some store traffic. To generate store sales, though, consider offering a discount or premium to the customers who make contributions to the program at your store. To add some excitement to the promotion, offer to make a matching donation if the customer donates their discount to the cause!

Jingle bell coupon

The jingle bell coupon lets everyone have a little fun while encouraging holiday sales. During a given time period (no more than a week), every customer who comes into the store with a bell gets a discount—just like they were handing in a paper coupon clipped out of the newspaper. And just like a newspaper coupon, it can be limited to one per customer, apply to every purchase or just to certain items, and represent a price percentage or fixed amount.

Family album

To encourage multiple store visits during the holidays, decorate your store with pictures of their families drawn by your customers' kids. Print a simple page with a big area for the picture and a place for their name, address, and phone number. The customer picks up the form and takes it home for the little artist to fill out. Then they return it to the store for display on a wall or in a window. A few days before Christmas, all the pictures are thrown in a barrel and one is drawn to receive a present from you—a bike or a model car. And don't forget to add the names and addresses to your mailing list before you dispose of the pictures.

Newbie gift basket

Establishing a good relationship with a customer new to your market lays the foundation for future sales. First-time car owners, for example, are like first-time mothers—they need lots of stuff. Put together a first car gift package that contains a selection of standard items like a chamois, wash mitt, vinyl cleaner, ice scraper, etc., put a bow on it, and build a display. You might want to offer two or three packages at different price points. You can add extra value to the package at no cost to you by adding some coupons supplied by a stereo installer, car wash, gas station, or other complementary retailer interested in reaching a brand new customer. You can obviously do the same for first time home owners, parents, boat and RV buyers, or whatever market segment fits your business.

Santa contract

Crowded stores, no parking spaces, surly, overworked clerks...Ho! Ho! Ho! It's holiday shopping time! You can't do much about the first two problems, but the last one—your staff—is directly under your control. One way to combat lousy service is to offer the Santa Contract, which pledges that your personnel will provide a friendly hello, a cheerful attitude, helpful service and customer satisfaction. Put it in writing on counter cards, window posters, and lapel buttons. Then make sure everyone on your payroll knows why they're responsible for carrying it out. As an added incentive, you can ask customers to identify a "Santa" who was particularly helpful or cheery to receive a little something extra in their stocking this year.

Wrapping help

For many of us, gift-wrapping is like re-folding a road map; it's a good idea to find someone else to do it for you. You can probably make a few phone calls and find a school or church group to run a gift-wrap service for your business as a fund raiser. Even if it's only for a few days or during limited hours, it's a very welcome service especially attractive to male customers. We guys especially need gift-wrapping help, by the way, since we have no experience what-so-ever in using road maps. Who needs 'em?

White sale

Hopefully, holiday sales don't end completely on December 24. To keep the traffic going into the new year, hold a white sale, just like most department stores do in January. Instead of selling sheets and towels, though, put promotional prices on merchandise that is white. And a final holiday sales suggestion: don't discourage returns and exchanges—promote them! Remember, every time you get the customer into the store, you have a chance to sell them something else.

Like all promotions, these take a little extra work and a few entail some expense. But one or more of them can help you boost sales during that important year-end holiday period.

About Dave Donelson

I've had four careers—each building on the one that came before it. The first was in small-market radio and television where I did everything from reporting the news and writing ad copy to selling spot schedules to local businesses. In the process, I learned a ton about how small companies work, how they interact with their customers, and what kinds of challenges they face—not just advertising and marketing problems, but personnel, finance, real estate, insurance, and even succession planning.

My second career was in national ad sales. I honed my selling skills competing for million-dollar budgets spent by the largest advertisers in the world. In addition to working with them and their advertising agencies on locally-executed campaigns in markets around the country, I built management skills as I climbed the ladder to eventually establish and run a nationwide sales organization with eleven offices and several hundred sales and support personnel.

Having built a company from the ground up for someone else, I decided it was time to strike out on my own, an urge that led me to found Sales Development Associates, Inc. (Donelson SDA), a management consulting firm that specialized in helping companies that were going through ownership changes and strategic transitions. My clients included one of every seven commercial television stations in the U.S. as well as companies in fields as diverse as heavy manufacturing and construction, magazine publishing, industrial sales, retail operations, and consumer services. I also took advantage of several opportunities to further test my entrepreneurial mettle by investing in a few select client companies and several successful start-ups.

Those investments allowed me to start my fourth career. For the last several years, I've been a writer and speaker, sharing what I learned with readers of some three dozen national newspapers and magazines and audiences at trade associations, professional group club meetings, and conventions of state and national organizations. In addition to the Dynamic Manager series, I'm the author of *Creative Selling: Boost Your B2B Sales* (Entrepreneur Press, 2000), and two novels. Learn more about me and the Dynamic Manager series at www.thedynamicmanager.com.

An excerpt from

The Dynamic Manager's Guide To Creative Selling:
How To Find New Customers
And Sell More To The Ones You Have
by Dave Donelson

Add-On Selling:
How to Turn A Good Sale Into A Great Sale

Even in this day of on-line price-driven shopping, brick-and-mortar retailers actually have a big tactical advantage—their ability to interact face-to-face with customers in real time. Not only does that mean the customer's needs are better met, but the shop owner has an opportunity to persuade the customer to buy something additional on the spot.

Sure, web programmers have developed gimmicks to encourage add-on sales like Amazon.com's "Other Customers Who Bought X Also Bought Y" algorithm, but that's not nearly as effective as an appliance store sales person looking the customer in the eye and saying, "you'd really get the most out of that range if you added this mid-top grill." The back-and-forth and give-and-take with the customer presented by such opportunities is invaluable when it comes to building the dollar volume of each individual transaction.

Back in the good old days, when retail stores had salespeople to help customers choose their merchandise, it was standard procedure to try to increase the size of each individual sale. They did this very effectively in several ways and many of them can be adopted by sharp contemporary retailers who are interested in increasing the top line on their income statements.

One of the first is simple up-selling, where you guide the customer to a selection with a higher price point than the one they came in to buy. To use an extreme example, let's say you are an auto parts retailer and a customer comes to your shop for a bottle of fuel injector cleaner. Instead of just ringing up the $4.99 sale, a dedicated up-seller would attempt to sell him a whole new fuel injection system instead. By asking a few questions about the problem the customer is trying to solve with the cleaner, the seller at least opens the door to a sale a hundred times larger. Outlandish? Maybe, but you never know until you try. And, as long as the suggestion is done quickly and without pressure, the customer won't mind.

A good way to manage this kind of interchange with the customer is to ask them what problems they're having while you're getting the item they came in for. That's also the time to get some basic information like what kind of car they're working on so you can give them an accurate quote. Then, even if they say "no thanks" to the suggestion, you can reply with "Let me at least give you a price so you can think about it." There's no pressure on the customer in up-selling this way.

Add-ons

Another sales-building strategy is to suggest add-ons to the original purchase. Back when shoe stores had salespeople who actually helped you find the right size and style, you couldn't buy a pair without the salesperson offering you some socks, shoe trees, and a jar of polish. Just about any retailer can and should do the same thing. Once you've sold the customer a sofa, for example, that's the time to suggest a pair of end tables and maybe some lamps.

Adds-ons should be, but don't necessarily have to be, related in some way to the customer's original purchase. The also usually have a lower price point. They are truly impulse purchases for the customer, although the impulse arises when the salesperson mentions the possibilities.

There is no reason these same tactics can't work for service revenues, too. The customer that has you install a set of adjustable shocks on their car might also be interested in an undercoating job, for example. One incentive for the customer to make the additional purchase might be that you can save him or her some money by doing both jobs at the same time. It can also save the customer something else that's valuable—their time.

Up-sell bargain hunters, too

There are some situations where you might think that up-sells and add-ons aren't possible, like when a bargain-hunting customer comes into the shop and says, "I'm looking for such-and-such, and I only want to spend X dollars." There are several ways to deal with that kind of low-baller. The first is to call their bluff and see how serious they are about their budget by telling them you don't have anything in that price range and offering to show them secondhand merchandise or a cheaper job. Note that you're not refusing to meet their needs, just their price. You're also sending them a not-so-subtle message that their expectations may be too high without telling them flat out that they're an idiot.

Another way is to just ignore what they say about their budget and start at the high end of the market and work your way down. One advantage of this approach is that it gives the customer a chance to see options they might not even know exist. What's more, after they've tasted that royal banana split, it makes their plain vanilla cone look a whole lot less appealing.

Yet a third approach is to give them alternatives and let them choose. Even if Product A and Product B are both priced higher than they say they are willing to pay, it's always very possible that their budget will change if you do a good job of selling the features and benefits of the higher-priced options. This is also a good way to find out what's really important to them, both in terms of what they are looking for and how much they are really willing to pay.

Sell the right thing

A similar customer with pricing on the mind may insist they can get by with a cheaper product even when you know they are ultimately going to be dissatisfied with it. It's important to sell this customer the right product the first time if at all possible, because they will probably blame you for their dissatisfaction later—even if you sold the cheap product to them under protest. Even worse, they may spread the bad word to their friends. Selective memory is a powerful force for evil.

One way to up-sell them is to play up the differences between the cheaper and the better products while you stress the very small differential in their prices by breaking it down into smaller amounts. Over the life span of two brands of high performance tires, for example, how many pennies per mile does the price difference amount to?

Seller reluctance

You and your estimators or other salespeople may be reluctant to use these tactics because of expected customer resistance or even resentment. But as long as you watch how they are reacting, listen to what they're saying to you, and don't try to cram something down their throat, that problem won't be nearly as bad as you think. Remember, you're dealing with somebody who has already decided to spend some money with you, so they're must be pretty comfortable with the way you do business. They've also demonstrated their mindset to buy, so you're not asking them to do something that's against their nature.

The biggest obstacle to increasing your sales this way, however, is simple laziness. It's a lot easier to just give the customer what they ask for, take their money, and say goodbye. When you do that, though, you've just obliterated the advantage your brick-and-mortar location has over the on-line drop shipper you compete with.

You're also doing the customer a disservice because you can't be sure that what you sold them will really meet their needs. How much do they know about what they are buying? Do they really understand what alternatives they have or what the differences are between various products? Add-on selling is a good way to get to know what they truly need, which puts you--the professional—in a position to make sure they buy the right thing.

When you understand it that way, you realize that you are creating value for the customer while you are bringing more dollars into your business. That's about the best formula for success I've heard since someone advised me to buy low and sell high.

Coming in 2011

The Dynamic Manager's Guide To Creative Selling:
How To Find New Customers
And Sell More To The Ones You Have
by Dave Donelson

also by Dave Donelson . . .

The Dynamic Manager's Guide To Marketing:
How To Create And Nurture Your Best Customers

If you want to grow your business, add "People" to Product, Price, Place, and Promotion, the classic elements of marketing. Attracting their attention, persuading them to buy from you, and ensuring their satisfaction with your product or service all require good people skills. Dave Donelson shows you how to develop and apply those skills in The Dynamic Manager's Guide To Marketing. Learn what makes your customers tick, why they buy from you—or your competitors, and how to make them your customers for life.

ISBN 978-1-4524-4499-4
Amazon Kindle ASIN B0044XV0R6

Available for all ebook readers from your favorite ebook vendor. Audiobook edition read by the author available from Audible.com and iTunes.

www.thedynamicmanager.com

Please note: this is Section One of **The Dynamic Manager's Guide To Marketing & Advertising.**

also by Dave Donelson . . .

The Dynamic Manager's Guide To Advertising:
How To Grow Your Business With Ads That Work

Effective small business advertising isn't impossible, it's just hard. It's hard to make good ads, to buy efficient media, to judge results. But it's not impossible. Dave Donelson shows you how to grow your business in **The Dynamic Manager's Guide To Advertising**. Learn how to attract new customers, build loyalty, encourage repeat purchases, and increase your share of the market with advertising techniques practiced by real small businesses just like yours.

ISBN 978-1452491011
Amazon Kindle ASIN B003X9786Y

Available for all ebook readers from your favorite ebook vendor. Audiobook edition read by the author available from Audible.com and iTunes.

www.thedynamicmanager.com

Please note: this is Section Two of **The Dynamic Manager's Guide To Marketing & Advertising.**

also by Dave Donelson . . .

Heart Of Diamonds
A novel of love, scandal, and death in the Congo

Corruption at the highest levels of government, greed in the church, and brutality among warring factions make the Congo a very dangerous place for television journalist Valerie Grey. Amid the bloody violence of that country's endless civil war, Grey uncovers a deadly diamond-smuggling scheme that reaches from the heart of the Congo to the White House by way of an American televangelist. **Heart Of Diamonds** is a fast-paced tale of ambition, avarice, betrayal, and love.

*"An absolutely brilliant must-read book. Dave Donelson captures the essence of the Congo's challenges. His **Heart Of Diamonds** is the modern corollary to Joseph Conrad's **Heart of Darkness**. Dave breaks the silence about the conflict in the Congo and firmly stands with the Congolese people in their quest for peace, justice, and human dignity."*

> --*Kambale Musavuli, National Spokesperson, Friends of the Congo.*

ISBN 978-1449919924
Amazon Kindle ASIN B0032UY4UM

www.heartofdiamods.com

Available for all ebook readers from your favorite ebook vendor.
Audiobook edition read by the author available from Audible.com and iTunes.

also by Dave Donelson . . .

Hunting Elf
A doggone Christmas story

A puppy for Christmas? What could be better! Dan McCoy and his capable wife June find out when Santa gives them a frolicsome hairball named Elf, a Silky Terrier with champion bloodlines and the table manners of Groucho Marx at a Hunter S. Thompson New Year's Eve party. He's also on the wish list of nefarious dognappers who want to steal him as part of a murderous plot to win Westminster's "Best In Show." Elf foils everybody's plots, though, and brings Macy's Thanksgiving Day Parade to a tumultuous halt in the process. Hunting Elf is a comedic canine Christmas adventure.

"Donelson fills the novel with experiences recognizable by anyone who has ever raised a puppy. Elf lifts his leg in all the wrong places, chews on everything from an heirloom Oriental carpet to the CATV cable, and has an uncontrollable urge to dig up and eat delicacies like kitty paté, which gives a whole new meaning to the term 'doggie breath.'"
                                                                                          --The Larchmont Gazette

ISBN 978-1456315924
Amazon Kindle ASIN B000ZM2HO0

www.huntingelf.com

Available for all ebook readers from your favorite ebook vendor.
Audiobook edition read by the author available from Audible.com and iTunes.

One of the few things I enjoy as much as writing is speaking before groups of all kinds.
--Dave Donelson

"Wow! What a great presentation you made at our Annual Convention last week! We've heard excellent remarks and compliments on your session and hope you enjoyed doing it at least half as much as our delegates enjoyed hearing you."

--Oscar Rodriguez, Deputy Director Texas Association of Broadcasters

"Your seminar was great. Everyone in attendance seemed to enjoy themselves and I continue to hear very positive comments about your presentation. You were successful at interjecting some fun into the day, as well as providing our members with some very useful and much needed information."

--Sue Toma, Executive Director, Iowa Broadcasters Association

"...a timely and compelling presentation. Our evaluations indicate that it ranked high above average. Some of the positive comments we received referred to your upbeat tone, humorous style, inspirational words, and thought-provoking presentation."

--Debbie Griffin, President DFW Society for Marketing Professional Services

For more information

Email dave@thedynamicmanager.com